GHOSTS & LEGENDS
OF
CRAWFORDSVILLE, INDIANA

CHRISTOPHER HUNT AND CHRISTINA HUNT

Haunted America

Published by Haunted America
A Division of The History Press
Charleston, SC
www.historypress.com

First published 2023

Manufactured in the United States

ISBN 9781467154680

Library of Congress Control Number: 2023937197

This is for my Grandma Gladys, who always believed in me and who was always there when I needed her. This is for my Uncle Dennis, who put that first fantasy novel in my hands as a little boy, opening my mind and heart to the wider world around me. Thank you to Charley for all the talks and discussions that helped shape my thoughts and brought me back to reality from some of my longer rabbit holes.
—Christopher

For Wesley and Michael, who love my ghost stories.
—Christie

CONTENTS

ACKNOWLEDGEMENTS

W hile the people we would like to thank and acknowledge for all their contributions to this book could quite possibly fill a whole book on its own, we would especially like to share our heartfelt gratitude to Dellie Craig of the Crawfordsville District Public Library for her endless patience with all our questions and rabbit hole digging; Karen Zach for her unending wisdom, guidance and amazing research resources (seriously, check out her website www.ingenweb.org/inmontgomery); Elizabeth Peck of the Old Jail Museum; Nolan Eller, Wabash archivist; Lucinda Brooks; Hanna Gray; Jim Boros of the Backstep Brewing Company; Jerry Turner for inspiration and amazing articles on Facebook: Montgomery County History and Folklore; Hoosier Chronicles for access to thousands of old newspaper articles; and every citizen of Crawfordsville who came forward with their own stories and family legends about the town.

We would also like to thank our families, friends, coworkers and random persons on the street who had to deal with our overly excited, eager digging into this wonderful city's rich history. We're sorry for any headaches, long nights or boring lectures you had to suffer through!

We also want to thank the great city of Crawfordsville itself. You are a part of every citizen who calls you home, and through you, we are all one family. Also, go Little Giants!

INTRODUCTION

Crawfordsville is located in the heart of Montgomery County, Indiana, and is the county seat. The first residents were William Offield and his wife, Jennie, who built their home on land near what is now Offield Creek in 1821. Their son was the first baby born in the county. Offield Monument marks the location of the field where their home once stood. However, Crawfordsville wasn't officially founded until 1832, and though the Offields were our first residents, the town was named after U.S. secretary treasurer William Crawford.

People have described Crawfordsville as having beauty that no other place in Indiana could rival, and it has been known to be called the Athens of Indiana due to its abundance of railroad systems and accessibility to other larger cities. Wabash College, one of only three remaining all-male liberal arts colleges in the country, was built in the town in 1832. The Rotary Jail Museum houses one of the only still-working rotary cell jails in existence. It was one of the first places basketball was ever played in Indiana. The first airmail delivery in Indiana was delivered in Crawfordsville by hot air balloon. Crawfordsville also has a rich history of famous inhabitants, including General Lew Wallace, who wrote *Ben-Hur* while he was here. It has also been home to Will Hays, Dick Van Dyke, Joseph Crane, Janet Lambert, Will Shortz and many others.

With all this history, it is no wonder that many legends and wonders have been passed down through the generations. Stories of ghosts, monsters and the unexplained pepper its timeline and fill us with a sense of curiosity and sometimes horror. This town—which once was known for its elaborate Halloween parties that filled the downtown streets with visitors for the Witches' Festival, welcomed spiritualists and mediums and claimed to see the first documented UFO in the United States—does not disappoint for the paranormally inclined seekers.

PART I

CRAWFORDSVILLE'S WONDROUS AND STRANGE CREATURE SIGHTINGS THROUGHOUT THE AGES

THE CRAWFORDSVILLE SKY MONSTER

Throughout the history of mankind, we have spent our lives looking up into the sky and wondering what is up there. Some have been lucky enough to see something, and a lot of those things that are seen are believed to be machines of some kind, but every once in a while, we hear a story about something different, something maybe even alive flying in the atmosphere above our heads.

Atmospheric beasts are thought to be creatures that live within our atmosphere, usually undetected by humans, and have been seen throughout the ages in various forms. Different people have varying ideas on what these things may be: UFOs, aliens, hallucinations, visions from beyond or a yet undiscovered species of our own. Ivan T. Sanderson wrote a book on this last theory that emphasizes that most UFOs are in fact low-density animals that are native to the clouds. Crawfordsville is home to one of the most famous atmospheric beasts of all time, known as the Crawfordsville Monster.

The first week of September 1891 was a bustling time for Crawfordsville. The county had just had its electric streetlights installed. The county fair was set to begin in two weeks, and it was a major event. At the time, Crawfordsville's county fair was an event rivaled only by the Indiana State Fair. The weather was starting to change from the heat of summer to the cooler, rainy weather of fall, and this small rural town was filled with people who felt safe and secure in their homes during the night. The early hours of September 5, 1891, changed all that feeling to one of terror and speculation.

Sometime in the early morning hours, Reverend G.W. Switzer stepped out of his home to fetch a drink at the well in the backyard, and there he witnessed a sight no one would ever forget. When he later recounted the tale to local newspapers, he said he felt a strange sensation come over him before looking up into the night sky. There he saw a creature swimming through the air over the church. He claimed it looked like floating drapery, at least sixteen feet long and eight feet wide. He called out to his wife, and she, too, saw the creature. They watched it hover over the church before descending toward the road and rising back up into the sky.

Crawfordsville Daily Journal, *September 7, 1891*
Mr. Switzer Saw the Spook
He Beholds the Midnight Wraith Which Alarmed Mr. Martin's Ice Men.
It seems that Marshall McIntyre and Bill Gray were not the only witnesses of the mysterious apparition which hovered over our city from midnight on Friday on till the dawn of Saturday morning. Several others witnessed the ghostly visitor and were also completely mystified both by its appearance and its actions. Rev. G.W. Switzer, of the Methodist church, saw it, and his story is rather interesting. Shortly after midnight he stepped into his back door yard to get a drink at the well. As he stood there a strange weird sensation crept over him and although he is unable to say whether he was attracted by any sound or not he suddenly felt his attention drawn upward, and raising his eyes with the full expectation of beholding something, he saw what both puzzled and astonished him. The night was very dark and very still, no breath of air stirring, but propelled by some unseen force he saw sweeping toward him from the southwest the apparition. It was about sixteen feet long and eight feet wide, resembling a mass of floating drapery. "Shaped like a fleecy, milk white cloud or like a demon in a shroud." It was much too low to be a cloud and moved far too swiftly, besides there was no wind at all. It seemed to work about as, it swam through the air in a writhing, twisting manner similar to the glide of some serpents. Mr. Switzer called his wife out and they watched it until got just east of the church when it began to descend as though about to land in the yard of Mrs. J.M. Lane. They then lost sight of it for the moment, but Mr. Switzer proceeding into the street saw it arise again and he and his wife then watched it circle about town for some time, finally tiring and going into the house with the strange phenomenon still visible. Mr. Switzer is wholly unable to account for it but is satisfied that it was not the Shawnee Mound ghost. V.Q. Irwin

says that it was a spirit, while the unkindest remark of all was made by Prof. Robert Burton who gravely gives as his opinion that it was "a delusion which got on the optic nerve of those men who had probably been imbibing intoxicants."

That same day, around two o'clock in the morning, Marshall McIntyre and Bill Gray were preparing to start their workday. They were at the barn of their employer, Mr. Martin, on Green Street, hitching up their team and wagon before getting ready to haul ice. They, too, felt a strange sensation come over them, akin to awe and dread. When they looked into the western sky, they saw the creature, about one hundred feet above ground, moving rapidly through the air.

They described the creature much as Reverend Switzer had, except they added it seemed to have several fins it used to move through the sky and no discernible head. They watched it in abject terror circle above them and move off toward the eastern sky only to return to hover over them again. Frightened for their safety, the men took shelter in the barn until the creature flew off again.

Crawfordsville Daily Journal, *September 5, 1891*
A Strange Phenomenon
A Horrible Apparition Hovers over the City at an Early Hour this Morning. What Tam O'Shanter saw on his famous ride was discounted this morning about two o'clock by what Marshall McIntyre and Bill Gray saw. They were at that hour at the barn of William Martin on East Main Street, hitching up the team to the ice wagon preparatory to leaving for the ice houses. While standing in the alley back of the stable Mr. McIntyre suddenly felt a strange sensation of awe and dread coming over him and looking up he saw a horrible apparition approaching from the west. It was about three or four hundred feet in the air, and most gruesome in aspect. It was about eighteen feet long and eight feet wide and moved rapidly through the air by means of several pairs of side fins which it worked most sturdily. It was pure white and had no definite shape or form, resembling somewhat a great white shroud fitted out with propelling fins. There was no tail or head visible but was one great flaming eye, and a sort of a wheezing, plaintive sound was emitted from a mouth which was invisible. It flapped like a flag in the winds as it came on and frequently gave a great squirm as though suffering unutterable agony. When it came to be directly over the residence of Mr. Martin it began to sweep slowly

and majestically around in a circle. It hovered thus for some time and the watchers fearing lest it was after their bacon retired for safety to the shelter of the barn. The apparition finally flew off toward the east, but when it reached the city limits it returned and began again to hover over Mr. Martin's house. Mr. McIntyre was in favor of rousing the family but his companion interposed his objection so the men watched it alone until after three o'clock whey they drove off to the ice house leaving the spook or whatever it was still hovering high in the air. It remained there as long as they could see its position but was gone when they returned at daylight. Both of them are much worked up over the affair and very naturally associate it with the supernatural. They will carry a Springfield rifle to the barn the next time they go and if the apparition again comes flapping around they will drill a hole in him with an ounce of cold lead.

Over the course of this weekend, over one hundred residents of Crawfordsville witnessed this creature. Most of them recalled the weird sensations washing over them before the creature appeared, and others also noted that birds around town seemed to make distress calls to one another as the beast moved around. There are reports of the creature giving off a strange heat and an almost mechanical wheezing noise, while others claim a flaming singular eye could be seen.

While we can never be sure what exactly these people saw in the sky, there is no doubt they did see something they couldn't explain. There were two men who came forward a few weeks after the incident who claimed it was nothing more than a flock of killdeer moving through the sky, but other residents claimed these two were known as local drunks and liars and were seeking their fifteen minutes of fame.

The extremely famous (at the time) Charles Fort was a paranormal writer and was convinced this story was made up and that Reverend Switzer didn't really exist. To prove his point, he looked into the matter and found that the reverend did exist, so he wrote to him asking for his story. Unfortunately, the reverend was traveling at the time and died before he was able to send his story to Fort. Charles Fort later wrote about the Crawfordsville Monster in his book *LO!*

LO! by Charles Fort
Brooklyn Eagle, Sept. 10 1891—something that was seen, at Crawfordville, Indiana, 2 A.M., Sept. 5th. Two icemen saw it. It was a seemingly headless monster, or it was a construction, about 20 feet

long, and 8 feet wide, moving in the sky, seemingly propelled by fin-like attachments, it moved toward the icemen. The icemen moved. It sailed away, and made such a noise that the Rev. G.W. Switzer, pastor of the Methodist church, was awakened, and, looking from his window, saw the object circling in the sky. I suppose that there was no such person as the Rev. G.W. Switzer. Being convinced that there had probably never been Rev. G.W. Switzer, of Crawfordsville—and taking for a pseudo-standard that if I'm convinced of something that is something to suspect—I looked him up. I learned that Rev. G.W. Switzer had lived in Crawfordsville, in September, 1891. Then I found out his present address in Michigan. I wrote to him, and received a reply that he was traveling in California, and would send me an account of what he had seen in the sky, immediately after returning home. But I have been unable to get him to send that account. If anybody sees a "headless monster" in the sky, it is just as well to think that over, before getting into print. Altogether, I think that I make here as creditable and scientific a demonstration as any by any orthodox scientist, so far encountered by us. The problem is: Did a "headless monster" appear in Crawfordsville, in September, 1891? And I publish the results of my researches: "Yes a Rev. G.W. Switzer did live in Crawfordsville at the time."

Years after the "Sky Monster" was seen, Vincent Gaddis, a writer for the Fortean Society, founded by those who were fans of Charles Fort, became interested in this tale and came to Crawfordsville to interview the people who had seen the beast. He quickly became obsessed with the notion of this creature and wrote on it many times in his life. His work isn't the only noteworthy telling of Crawfordsville's most famous cryptid, as there was also a graphic novel published featuring the sky monster.

Mysterious Fires and Lights, *by Vincent Gaddis*

In such observations as that of the Bonham (Texas) "eel" and similar "sky serpents" reported at other locations, the appearances, resembled clouds, but were "perfect in form" and in one case "moved with a hissing sound." The best detailed example of this type of appearance from my own files is the "sky monster" that frightened residents of Crawfordsville, Indiana, in September 1891. Having attended college and worked as a reporter in the vicinity of Crawfordsville, I had the opportunity to interview surviving witnesses and to read the original on the scene newspaper accounts of this astonishing visitation. Here are my notes as I wrote them at the Time:

Self-luminous, surrounded by an aura of dim white light, the appearance resembled "a white shroud with fins."

Doubt

Indiana's Sky Monster

Fifty-four years ago a large and mysterious object appeared in the sky over Crawfordsville, Ind. A brief account of the occurrence taken from the Brooklyn Eagle *(Sept 10, 1891) will be found in THE BOOKS OF CHARLES FORT (p. 637). The writer, residing close to the scene of this occurrence and having access to newspaper files containing a direct report from a Crawfordsville correspondent, adds the following notes to the published account: Self-luminous, or surrounded by an aura of dim white light, the object resembled "a white shroud with fins." No clear-cut shape or outline could be observed. It was about 18 or 20 feet long, eight feet wide, and no "head" or "tail" was visible. It moved rapidly, "like a fish in water" with the aid of "side fins." At times it flapped its fins with rapid motions. Emitting a wheezing, plaintive sound, it hovered about 300 feet above the surface most of the time, but several times it came within a hundred feet of the ground. All reports refer to this object as a living thing, but it could have been a construction. A flaming, red "eye" (or light) was noticeable. At times it "squirmed as if in agony." Once it swooped low over a group of witnesses who reported that it radiated a "hot breath." This visitor from the void made its appearance for two successive nights, Sept. 4–5, 1891, first coming into view about midnight on both nights, and disappearing upward about 2 a.m. On the first night the Rev. G.W. Switzer, pastor of the local Methodist Church, and his wife, watched the sky phantom for over an hour. Although Charles Fort confirmed this statement, he was never able to obtain a detailed report from Rev. Switzer. On the second night several hundred residents of the town watched the monster as it moved slowly over various parts of the business district for two hours. On the third night almost every adult in the town waited for its appearance, but it never came. Many remained up all night, only to be disappointed. The monsters appearance was strictly localized to the sky over Crawfordsville. The writer carefully checked all Indiana news dispatches for six months preceding an following this appearance, but no additional information or reports can be found.*

On September 4–6, 1891, something was seen in the skies over this town. It has several points that stand out: the red flaming eye, hovering for extremely long periods and the fact that it showed up two nights in a row like clockwork. There are lots of other things about its description that make the theory of it being a flock of killdeer highly unlikely, but those three are the biggest standouts. What was this thing? A creature, a machine or something we as of yet have no name for?

THE GIANT GRAVEYARD

There were giants in the earth in those days; and also after that, when the sons of God came in unto the daughters of men, and they bore children to them, the same became mighty men which were of old, men of renown.
—Genesis 6:4

Throughout history, we have been told stories and legends about creatures of gigantic size. The stories tell us that at one time, everything was larger on our planet, from animals to plants. So it isn't that far of a stretch to imagine that there would be a gigantic humanoid as well. According to the legends, the giants are human-like in appearance but are simply of larger stature and greater strength. The giants may be wild in appearance or nobler looking. Some legends even say they have supernatural powers.

The word *giant* comes from Robert of Gloucester's chronicle in 1297 and is also derived from the Greek word *gigantes*. Fairy tales have been made about them in modern times telling us they are monsters that only think about the basic instincts of survival: kill and eat or be killed and eaten. Throughout our history though, they have been thought of in many different ways, such as the Nephilim, Cyclops, Titans, Jötnar, Fomorians, Ogres and Asuras. Some were worshiped as gods, and others were fought as enemies of life.

The Bible tells us many tales of giants, starting with the Nephilim, the sons of fallen angels. The Nephilim were believed to be either the sons of fallen angels or the offspring that came from the children of Seth and

The Giants Bluff as it stands today. *Photo by authors*.

Cain mating. Either way, they were believed to be larger and stronger than humans. They were noble in form and in some cases so large as to blot out the sun. According to the Bible, they were one of the reasons God sent the flood during the time of Noah.

The Bible also tells us stories about Joshua and his fights with the Anakim. The Anakim were beings who lived in the southern part of Canaan. Their larger forms filled most of the Israelites with terror. The Israelites believed them to be the descendants of the Nephilim. Joshua finally banished them from the land except for a few that found homes with the Philistines. One such being was the giant Goliath, who fought David. David is said to have defeated the giant, showing that he was more fit to rule than the current ruler of Israel, Saul. This story is used often in modern times to show that the underdog can win if they work hard enough.

Greek mythology gives us stories about the Cyclops. Cyclops were giants who had only one eye. There were three groups of them. The three who were rescued by the god Zeus crafted his thunderbolt for him, which allowed him the power to defeat his enemies. The many different tales have them working for the god Hephaestus afterward. In Homer's *Odyssey*, we have Odysseus meeting the sons of Poseidon, who were one-eyed giants who ate men. The Cyclops he met were uncivilized shepherds who ate any man who stepped foot on their island. The third and final type was the Cyclopean wall builders. They were said to have built the walls of Mycenae, Tiryns and Argos.

The great Titans were the gods before the gods. They gave birth to Zeus and his family and were soon after overthrown by them. They towered as tall as the sky and gave birth to many things on the planet. Their leader Cronos murdered his own father, Uranus, in his bid to rule. He was in turn overthrown by his son Zeus, and so the circle kept going. They were imprisoned below the earth, in Tartarus, after the war.

The Norse people believed in giants that were in contrast to their gods. They were the gods' opposite and had the same powers. The largest and first was the giant Ymir, who gave birth to the others. He was killed by the first gods, and from his body was created the earth. They take many forms and are called different names depending on their form: frost giants, fire giants and mountain giants. They are believed to be who Odin and the gods will fight during Ragnarok, the battle believed to destroy the world.

The Fomorians are a supernatural race in Irish legend. They are mostly believed to be hostile and monstrous creatures. They come from under the sea or earth originally. They battled against the Tuatha Dé Danann and were defeated at the Battle of Mag Tuired. The story has a lot of similarities to the stories of the battles between Zeus and Cronos and even Odin and the frost giants. They represent chaos and all the bad things that happen.

In Europe, they sometimes call giants Ogres. Ogres are giants that are more monstrous in form and are cannibals. Ogres are in many fairy tales and usually are used to describe a large stupid creature that eats people as often as possible. They are ugly to look at and are usually solitary beasts. In Hindu, they are called Asuras, demigods with both good and bad personalities. Depending on the Indian story about them, they could be just a spirit that leads you down the wrong path or an evil so strong that they are considered anti-gods.

We tell these stories to scare ourselves and to warn about doing immoral things, but what if some of those stories come with a grain of truth? What if there really were giants among men in our past? And what if that past isn't as long ago as people may think? Across the world, we have lots of stories of gigantic humans and even stories of remains being found. Somehow, all these stories end with the remains being lost or destroyed. We even have a story right here in Crawfordsville about a giant graveyard that was found and excavated back in 1892.

Daily Journal, *October 20, 1892*
Remains of a Race of Giants Unearthed Crawfordsville Ind.
The employees of George Britton Crawfordsville, while at work on a gravel-pit discovered an old Indian cemetery, and have already taken out nearly thirty skeletons in an excellent state of preservation. Owing to their being buried in gravel. The bodies had all been buried in a sitting position with their hands raised and facing the west. The skulls show almost an entire absence of forehead and the implements found do not correspond with any seen before. Some of the men must have been a full 7 feet high, and the opinion is advanced by local archeologists that the skeletons are the remains of a race which occupied this region previous to the Ouiatonon or Wabash Indians.

The date was, as near as can be found, October 14, 1892. This site was strange because it was in a gravel pit. The gravel allowed the skeletons to stay in extremely good condition with little to no decay even though it had been a very long time since the bodies were placed there. The teeth were in such a good state that some still retained enamel.

Some scientists who visited the area dated the skeletons to be at least two hundred years old but found they could easily be as much as four hundred years old. We have different reports saying anywhere from twelve to thirty skeletons were removed from the site in just over a week's time. There were some reports that little to no artifacts were recovered outside of antler tips, but other reports speak of artifacts being found that didn't fit known periods at the time, including pottery and some copper. The archaeologists working the site said they had never seen such strange-looking implements and types of pottery.

As strange as this story may seem, it is truly only the tip of the iceberg. The bodies were found in a sitting position with their hands raised, and they all faced the west. Several of the skeletons reached over seven feet in height. The bodies were a mixture of men, women and even children. They were all showing peculiarities in form both in height and in how their skulls were shaped. They were abnormally large compared to a modern man's.

Daily Argus, *October 21, 1892*
Gruesome Relics
The teamsters, who are hauling from the gravel pit on the west side of the city, still continue to unearth human skeletons but visitors are on the spot and carry off the bones and relics almost as fast as they are uncovered. Many

are superstitious, however, and will not touch them under any consideration. Yesterday afternoon some curiosity seekers, who were prospecting about the bank dug up a skull, which was absolutely perfect and with every tooth intact. Some of the skulls, it has been noticed, are almost without forehead and the skull tapers back from the eyes. In this particular case, however, there was a high commanding brow and if the size of the cranium is any criterion, he must have possessed a mighty intellect. A student, free from anything resembling superstition or dread of the supernatural was struck by the fact and placed his hat, size seven, on the skull but it was altogether too small and in the life the gentleman must have worn a number eight or nine head dress.

One of the men working the site attempted to put his size-seven hat on one of the skulls and found that the skull was one to two sizes larger at least. A size-eight hat is three times a normal person's hat size. The skulls show almost an entire absence of a forehead and taper back from the eyes. They had high, commanding brows and extra-large craniums.

Unfortunately, the bones and other relics were just thrown out of the pit onto the hillside for anyone to take. Most of those hanging around were relic hunters and superstitious crap shooters in search of strange items. After examining the skeletons, Dr. Decaux Tilney, Dr. Gott and other local physicians believed the bodies to be those of a race of white people instead of Native Americans, as was first thought.

Daily Journal, *October 22, 1892*
A Gruesome Mystery
Dr. Decaux Tilney has consulted with Dr. Gott and other local physicians and has come to the conclusions that the skeletons being exhumed on the farm of George Britton are not those of Indians but of whites. The process by which the amiable doctor makes this deduction and reaches this truly admirable conclusion is one which calls for the plaudite of his fellow man. The doctor exhibited a heel bone which one of his boys had brought home from the cemetery to throw at the chickens and stray dogs, and also displayed the pelvic bone of an infant which had evidently died before attaining to the age of accountability. Dr. Tilney argues that both of these bones were those of persons of nervous temperament and hence not Indians. This information is valuable to the students of archeology and will go far toward solving the mystery. Dr. Tilney believes the bones to be those of murdered whites and the Indian relics are mere little accidents.

So, who were they? What were they? Were they simply Native Americans who passed on and were buried in the area, or were they something else, something older and still undiscovered? Were they members of that race that we only know of as the mysterious mound builders? We even now find ourselves discovering more and more humanoid races that dwelled on our planet many ages ago.

> Crawfordsville Review, *October 29, 1892*
> *The Gravel Pit Grave Yard*
> *Skeletons continue to be turned up by the spades in the gravel pit on the farm of George Britton. On Tuesday five skeletons were taken from the gravel pit and several more since then. Altogether over thirty skeletons have been exhumed and many of them carried off by relic hunters. No stone axes, pipes, or arrow heads have as yet been unearthed. To what race or nation these remains belong is a question puzzling many people and bids fair to remain unanswered. Many consider them as belonging to the Indians who roamed over this portion of the country in the early part of the century and for ages previous, others that they belonged to some early explorers who may have had their camp or village there. Another theory is that these remains were those of the Mound Builders, or ancient Aztecs, who are known to have inhabited this country centuries ago. On the Cope farm a half mile north of the gravel pit, and on the south side of the river is a structure of earth about 80 feet long, 20 feet or more in height, which is undoubtedly the work of the Mound Builders. All persons who have visited it pronounce it such. It may be that this earth work and the burying ground on the Britton farm were used by the same people, and that at an early period a town was located in that vicinity.*

Who says science is right and that they all died out and some didn't live until closer to our own time? The skulls' description is very similar to other races of humanoids that have been found in recent years, most notably the dragon man skull. If we are still finding new races of people to this very day, how can we say that they weren't something bizarre or strange such as a race of giants on the earth? As we discover more about our history and the history of earth itself, this mystery may yet come to light. The size of these skeletons may make us speculate and wonder, but is it really so far-fetched that people could have been taller than average, maybe even giants?

There are legends of people who were two to three feet tall in several parts of the world, as well as people more than twenty-five feet. We have even today noticed that our average height seems to be going up in our own race. Seven feet is tall but is not even the tallest person in the world at the time of this discovery. That honor was held by a gentleman named John Rogan (1867–1905). He was eight feet, nine inches tall and the second-tallest man in history. It has often been seen in history that civilizations will breed for certain sought-after traits: longer necks, eye color or hair color and, yes, even height. Could this site have been a tribute to such a people? In this case, maybe it was the height that grew stronger through breeding with a limited number of individuals.

We have lots of legends of people finding large humans or giants throughout history. The Native Americans speak of different tribes of them they came across throughout history, some benevolent and others aggressive. Some were cannibals and some makers of things. Some legends even state the mound builders or other wonders of our ancient world were created by giants.

Many ancient civilizations tell stories of giants. Even some of our most famous explorers tell stories of giants from not too long ago. Ferdinand Magellan, one of the most well-known explorers in our history, has ties to a famous account of giants as told by a member of his crew, Antonio Pigafetta:

> But one day saw a giant, who was on the shore, quite naked, and who danced, leaped, and sang, and while he sang he threw sand and dust on his head. Our captain sent one of his men toward him, charging him to leap and sing like the other in order to reassure him and to show him friendship. Which he did. Immediately the man of the ship, dancing, led this giant to a small island where the captain awaited him. And when he was before us, he began to marvel and to be afraid, and he raised one finger upward, believing that we came from heaven. And he was so tall that the tallest of us only came up to his waist. Withal he was well proportioned.

So with all that we don't know about the history of the world and all that we are still discovering, could this be a case of mistaken identity, or could it have actually been a new kind of humanoid we had not then— or maybe even now—discovered? There are lots of different articles in newspapers throughout the state and other states on the giant graveyard discovery in Crawfordsville.

DEER MAN

T hroughout the history of the world, lots of myths, stories and legends have told of different types of half-human, half-animal hybrids. In Egypt, the monuments still show lots of pictographs of many different types of half-human creatures. Even their gods were known to have the heads of animals. In some lands and cultures, we have satyrs, which were half-goat and half-man; minotaurs, which were half-bull and half-man; and centaurs, which were half-horse and half-man. But in North America, we have legends of something a little different.

We have the cryptids known as the Deer Man, Deer Woman, Wendigo, Ljiraq or many other names depending on what part of North America you reside in; some even call it the Not Deer. Each has its differences and similarities. It always stands on two legs and has the body of a man. Some are believed to be supernatural in origin, while others are just creatures we have yet to discover with modern science.

The head changes depending on the part of the country you live in; it could be a deer, stag, elk, goat, bull or caribou, though the most commonly seen are stag or deer. The creature's legs seem to change from human to deer at will. Many are accompanied by a smell that changes depending on the witness. It may be a smell of rotting eggs, brimstone or a similar foul odor. Some of the creatures are believed to be benevolent, while others are thought to be darker or maybe evil.

Some sightings and legends tell that the Deer Man can change from a deer to a man or a hybrid at will and in a moment. Other stories tell how when it

The location of the Deer Man sighting. *Photo by authors.*

is in its true form, it is invisible to the eye or maybe just a spirit creature. It is usually described as being tall, upward of seven feet or even higher when it stands upright on two legs. Native Americans speak of the beings in hushed tones or with respect depending on the description, location and what was felt at the time of the sighting.

Could this cryptid be a Wendigo? The Wendigo is an interesting legend of an evil creature that can take different forms and in some legends is able to possess people. Might this creature be the legendary Ljiraq, a being believed to be human-like that could take the form of any animal it chose but preferred that of a caribou with a human face?

Then there is the Deer Woman. In some legends, it is believed to be a spirit of love and fertility. It is a great lover of women and children and will lure men who have harmed a woman or child to their deaths. The Deer Woman shows similarities and traits of both sirens and succubae, having an unnatural, alluring beauty until its prey is ensnared. While all these spirits will lure away and/or hurt others, they do have different features. The Deer Woman has hooves and antlers. Sirens are bird-like from the chest down. Succubae are said to be hideous and demonic but only after catching a person.

27

The Deer Man or Not Deer, as he is called in the Appalachian Mountains, is seen often in South Carolina; Virginia; Alberta, Canada; and other parts of North America. Crawfordsville has had its own sightings of the strange cryptid. Most of the sightings have been on the western edge of the city and stretch out into the western section of the county.

One such sighting, back in the winter of 1884, occurred when multiple men and women reported sighting the creature in the woods at night. Each person had a slightly different description of what they saw, but all agreed that it was unnaturally tall, seven feet at least, with deer-like horns, and a feeling of dread or fear permeated the area. They felt like the devil himself had come to Crawfordsville to haunt the area.

Another sighting, much closer to modern times, was had by a young woman and her friends. It was in the summer or fall of 2008 between 9:00 and 11:00 p.m. They were watching a movie in the living room of a house when suddenly a face was seen peering through the glass door. The glass on this door was well over six and a half feet off the ground when looking from outside. They all screamed, and the creature quickly disappeared from the glass. A few hours later, when the young woman was leaving to drive home, the creature was seen standing next to a sign by the road. The creature was tall enough to be level with the sign, which was at least seven feet off the ground. The antlers were like that of a deer, and there was a hint of fangs, but the eyes were the most striking and disturbing feature—predatory and watchful. She felt hunted when it looked at her.

One common description of the Deer Man, outside of its antlers, is of its eyes. The eyes are often reported as being red and some say glowing. When you look into its eyes, you feel like prey being watched for nefarious reasons. These sightings have been around for over a century and still are happening today, so it makes a person wonder what is out there in the night. Are the woods full of creatures we don't have names for, or are the ancient gods of the wild still at play, just out of eyesight?

BIGFOOT

Bigfoot—also commonly called Sasquatch, Yowie, Grassman, Skunk Ape, Yeti, Abominable Snowman and lots of other names—is an ape-like creature that inhabits the forests and mountains of the world. There are stories and sightings in most countries, and legends abound throughout the world's history. Famous explorer and mountaineer Sir Edmund Hillary even took on an expedition up Mount Everest in 1960 in search of proof of the Abominable Snowman. Some places, like Mount Everest, are more of a hotbed than others, and descriptions of the creature can vary drastically depending on the region you are in.

The name Bigfoot came from an event in 1958 involving Jerry Crew in Humboldt County, California. While working, he kept finding these gigantic footprints. Talking to his fellow workers proved that they had all been finding them for a while. Plaster casts were made and the story spread, and before too long, it was being talked about in the *New York Times* and *Los Angeles Times* newspapers. From that, the name Bigfoot stuck and would come to be used for an unknown creature leaving large footprints in rural parts of the country.

Bigfoot is usually described as a large, muscular, bipedal ape-like creature covered in earth-tone fur or hair. Its height has been placed between six and nine feet, with rare stories of it standing between ten and fifteen feet. Its weight can be as great as one thousand pounds. Its face varies, depending on the story, between looking more human or more ape.

Bigfoot sightings are as old as men existing on this continent, and many of the cultures across North America include tales of mysterious hair-covered wild men living in the deep forests. On the Tule River Indian Reservation in central California, there exists a site called Painted Rock. The site is believed to have been created by the Yokuts tribe between five hundred and one thousand years ago. The petroglyphs drawn there show what looks to be a group of Bigfoot called "the Family," and the locals call the largest of them the "Hairy Man."

Sixteenth-century explorers in California told tales of large creatures that stalked their camps at night. In Mississippi in 1721, there were reports of hairy creatures in the forests known to scream loudly and steal animals. The Sts'ailes people tell stories of a shapeshifting creature that protects the forest. The Iroquois tell tales of an aggressive, hair-covered giant. In 1847, Paul Kane told stories of a race of cannibalistic wild men living on the peak of Mount St. Helens. In the same area in 1924, a violent encounter happened between prospectors and ape men.

You can find sightings in every state and territory throughout the Americas. Most of the sightings are clustered in areas where deep forests or mountainous terrain is prevalent. One of the most famous sightings was the Patterson-Gimlin film, a very clear video of an ape-like creature moving through the woods. It was made in 1967 alongside Bluff Creek northwest of Orleans, California. The site is less than fifty miles from the Oregon border and less than twenty miles from the Pacific Ocean. Roger Patterson went to his grave claiming that the creature in the film was real and that none of the film was a hoax. Robert Gimlin kept out of the public eye for many years, refusing to give interviews, but maintained that he had never been involved in any part of a hoax with Patterson. In 2005, Gimlin finally began giving interviews and appearing at Bigfoot conferences to discuss the experience. He still claims that the creature was real and not a hoax.

There have been lots of hoaxes involved with the phenomenon but just as many, if not more, unexplained events and sightings. We know that the Native Americans described them as the giants of the wilderness or the wild men. They believed, for the most part, that they were kind creatures but could be terrors given the right provocation. Some pool the information that has been found and liken sightings of Bigfoot with other cryptid sightings such as Wendigo, dog man, giants and so on. But if you look at the trend of the sightings, you start to see that each of these cryptids are different and a species of their own.

Some believe that Bigfoot are spirits that exist to protect the wild country or were brought here by aliens or are aliens themselves. Others believe that they are interdimensional beings that just visit our plane of existence. Are they a bit of wishful thinking when we are out in the woods alone that some gentle giant is watching over us, or are they a horrible fear of what waits in the dark places when we are alone?

Indiana has been a hotbed of sightings of the creature for many years, especially Putnam County. So it isn't hard to believe that through the ages, we have had multiple sightings here in Crawfordsville and the surrounding area. One of the oldest sightings we have comes from January 1869.

Joseph Hardee was out coon hunting with a group when he came across a creature sitting in the middle of his path. The creature looked ape-like but was extremely large, and when Hardee approached, it let loose with a sound that was so terrific and appalling that it froze the blood in his veins. The creature beat on its chest with long arms. Hardee and his party, hearing the yell, made a quick retreat. Luckily, the animal showed no sign of following them. A group was closely assembled to hunt down the beast but had no luck finding it.

> *Fort Wayne, Indiana*
> Daily Democrat, *January 25, 1869*
> *The* Crawfordsville Review *tells a long and wonderful story of one Mr. Hardee, living in that vicinity, who, while out coon hunting, "was confronted by an appearance" which, he assured the editor, baffles description. By the light of his shell bark torch, it appeared like a gigantic ape, sitting in the path in front of him. What it was, he had no idea and the party being yet some distance in the rear, he hesitated about approaching it. His dog, meanwhile, crouched down at his feet, and refused to stir. Thinking it better to advance than retreat, Mr. H. waved his torch until it blazed brilliantly, and made a few steps towards the monster. When it uttered a yell so terrific and appalling, that it well nigh froze the blood in his veins. At the same time it seemed to beat upon its breast with long, uncouth arms. Mr. Hardee, although by no means lacking in courage, beat a hasty retreat. The remainder of the party, hearing the yell, had fled precipitately. The monster, animal, or whatever it was, did not, however, offer to pursue them. A party has been formed, to hunt down the monster some time during the present week. The* Review *adds: "Most of our readers are aware of the fact that the country where Mr. H. encountered the untamed monster is very wild and broken. It is on the route leading to the far-famed 'Shadow of Death,' that which a wilder or more desolate region is rarely to be found."*

This southwestern section of what was county and now is city is well known for sightings of the beast. There have been multiple accounts of people hearing calls and wood knocks. A story from the 1800s tells of men out foxhunting and coming across a large monstrous creature that had dark fur and smelled like a skunk. Yet another encounter took place just outside the city. The observer states that when it first started, they were sitting near a fire they had built in their yard and kept getting the feeling they were being watched. This was probably around 9:00 p.m. Their significant other asked them what was wrong, and they told him. A few minutes later, the cattle pastured behind the house started bawling and running like something either scared them or was chasing them. The significant other stepped out to the side of the garage (which was beside the house) and called to come look, and when they reached the spot and looked, they saw something tall standing in the moonlight. The significant other picked up a piece of steel pipe, his weapon of choice, and threw it at the shape, which didn't move.

They assumed it was a tree and went into the house shortly thereafter but couldn't shake the feeling of being watched. The next morning, when they went to investigate, they found the pipe but no tree or anything else in the area that could have been confused for what they saw. Where the pipe was found the next morning, the grass was all beat down and trails led through the pasture to where cattle were. There were two distinct trails. The grass was waist high, and you could tell that one was used as a path to come up and the other used to travel back by the way the grass lay. The weather was cool and clear, and there was a partial moon. These two felt certain there was nothing that they could have mistaken for the creature they believed they saw.

In another account, this same observer was going to bed late one night, and after they got settled in, they noticed every dog in the area barking like crazy. This wasn't normal, as the dogs were usually fairly quiet at night, hardly barking at all. Just as they were wondering what had stirred up the dogs so much, they heard a howl like they had never heard before. The best way they could describe it was like a low siren, but it sounded close. They lay there in the bed, frozen, wondering what it could be. They were familiar with all the wildlife in the area, as they had heard them plenty of times. Several years later, they came across a recording of the Ohio Bigfoot from 1994, and it was exactly the same sound. They had never heard it before or after.

In recent years, a theory has begun to take shape that maybe Bigfoot could be a hand-me-down version of an extinct species of ape called Gigantopithecus. This is just one of the many theories for what Bigfoot could be or be descended from. We may never know the truth, but many will continue the hunt to find out.

UFOs

Most of us have grown up with lots of books, movies, television shows and so on about UFOs (unidentified flying objects) or UAPs (unidentified aerial phenomenon), as they are now known, and stories fill up our minds and culture of alien beings coming down from the heavens to our world. These stories range from scary to funny or even romantic, but like most things in our history, we find that they come from a grain of truth. This is a phenomenon that has been hotly debated and researched for at least the last sixty years, and within the last couple of years, our government has opened up new discussions and released new evidence to support it and make us wonder, are we not alone in the universe?

UFOs/UAPs have been seen throughout the history of our modern world and some believe even our ancient one. History shows references to strange beings coming down from the skies to be worshiped as gods among men. Were these stories to teach us lessons, or were they accurate portrayals of beings coming to visit our planet and teach us things?

During World War II, round glowing fireballs, known as foo fighters, were seen in the skies by both the Allied and Axis fighter pilots. In 1946, thousands reported seeing unidentified objects flying over Scandinavian countries as well as France, Portugal, Italy and Greece. The most popular accounts may be from June 24, 1947, when a pilot named Kenneth Arnold reported seeing nine objects flying in formation over Mount Rainier in the United States. This report coined the phrase *flying saucer*, and off the tales went.

It seemed after those first few sightings—and a couple of crashes such as the Roswell incident and the Kecksburg incident—things got a little scarier. We begin finding reports of abductions by alien species and people having lost time. One of the first stories in the United States is the story of Barney and Betty Hill. The Hills were a married couple who believed that in September 1961, they were abducted by aliens. Today, hearing stories from people about being abducted is much more common, but during those days, it was rare.

What makes this story fascinating are all the details that were brought out and never disproven. The beings were said to be wearing black uniforms and caps and were somehow "not human." This immediately brings to mind stories of the men in black, who are said to be nearly human men who wear black suits and hats and visit many of those who have sightings of UFOs or aliens.

We have lots of stories about strange sightings and the creatures that accompany them. They can for the most part be divided up into categories such as disc, delta and tic tac–shaped UFOs. The creatures or aliens are a little harder to organize, but the most famous are the Grays, Nordic and Reptilians. You can find stories, legends and history of sightings everywhere in our world and history, even here in Crawfordsville. There have been multiple sightings throughout the history of our town; here are just a few of them as they are related to us.

National UFO Reporting Center
Occurred—2004, Reported—2006
Cigar shaped craft in Indiana—I was driving east on I-74 when my attention was caught by a group of birds flying. As I looked at the birds I noticed a bright white shape beyond them. It was cigar shaped and moving slowly from my right to left. It was about the size of my thumb with my arm extended. After about five seconds the left edge tilted downward slightly. Then the craft rotated, bringing the forward edge down and the rear edge up. This gave me a downward view at it. At this point it took on a circular shape. It then accelerated up and away from me at an incredible rate.

This story is interesting because it talks about the craft changing shape. Maybe there aren't different types at all; maybe the ships just change shape depending on what is needed at that moment, similar to how people have spoken about ships extending arms or landing gear right out of the side, as if the ship was growing at that moment and not like it came from a storage area.

There have been several sightings of cigar- or tic tac–shaped UFOs in the area over the years. Another sighting was reported by two women traveling down a road on the edge of the city. They saw what they described as a cigar-shaped craft flying along beside their car. They recalled that the craft had large windows and what looked like people standing inside and watching them.

The women immediately told their family but seemed to totally forget about the sighting afterward, even when asked. This continued until a drawing on a UFO documentary that happened to be playing on TV seemed to make it all rush back. They said the drawing of a cigar-shaped UFO was exactly what they saw and they were amazed with how much detail they remembered when just a few moments before they had no memory of what their family members had been talking about.

In 2012, the year many were convinced the world might end, thirteen red lights were seen flying above the Wabash campus in Crawfordsville. A similar phenomenon has spread across the world of seeing lights in formations flying through the sky. The Phoenix lights are probably the most famous sightings of this on record. Thirteen is also an interesting number, as it is tied to so many things paranormal.

> *National UFO Reporting Center*
> *Occurred—2012, Reported—2012*
> *Thirteen red lights travel same path over Wabash College—I was sitting on my front porch and looked up into the sky above Wabash College and thought I saw a plane—just looked like the red light but without the blinker. About 10 seconds later, another followed…and then another…and then another. Thirteen in all from the time I started counting, all following the same path. No sound of plane/jet engines and three simply disappeared (although they could have merely gone behind a cloud as it was partly cloudy that night).*

These are just a few stories from Crawfordsville about UFO sightings through the years. With the many other things seen in the skies of Crawfordsville, it makes you wonder how different the skies may be over this small town in the middle of America.

THE THUNDERBIRD

Native Americans in North America tell stories of enormous birds with wings so large that when they flapped, it created a noise like thunder. Some tribes took it a step further and said the creatures created thunder with their wings and shot lightning from their eyes. These birds are called by several names throughout the different tribes, but the most common in modern times is the Thunderbird.

The Thunderbird stories and legends go back to ancient days and continue all the way to modern times. One of the most famous stories comes out of Lawndale, Illinois, in 1977. Young Marion Lowe, a ten-year-old boy, was outside playing when he was attacked by a bird. The bird attempted to carry his body away. The boy's mother, seeing this, ran to his rescue, yelling and chasing the bird.

The bird dropped the boy and flew away. The incident was witnessed by multiple people. They described the bird as having four-foot wings, a four-and-a-half-foot body from beak to tail feather, a six-inch neck with a white ring around it and a hooked beak that was at least six inches. The whole creature was black except for a white ring. Some hunters trying to locate the creature found and destroyed extremely large nests.

Crawfordsville has had several sightings of extra-large birds, in some cases larger than a man standing upright. One story describes two young men playing on the edge of town when they were walking down a hillside. They noticed a noise and looked up to see a large bird flying down on them. They took off running to get to safety away from what they described as a huge bird.

Another sighting was witnessed by two people driving down the road in their truck. The bird flew above the truck for several minutes before flying off to a tree to sit. The bird was described as completely black, and its wings were so large they dwarfed the truck they were in.

This Is Indiana (thisisindiana.angelfire.com)
During early April 2021 in Crawfordsville, a woman was in a parking lot waiting for an appointment. Suddenly, a huge shadow like that of a small plane passed over her car. She was on the phone and told a friend about what she saw. She noticed through her windshield a huge bird that landed on an office roof. As she walked toward office she looked up and the huge bird looked down at her. It then flew down and glided toward her.

Are these birds of a lost species or even dinosaurs that haven't died out? Or are they just stories to scare us? At the end of the day, keep looking up and see what you can catch sight of.

FAIRY CREATURES

Throughout our childhoods, we hear stories about fairies and the fairy world. There are as many types of fairies as there are stars in the skies, it seems. When we grow up with these stories, we first believe in them and then later find out they were to be used as ways to warn a person away from immoral things. They teach and comfort us in strange ways.

But what if they aren't just stories? What if the fairy world exists and what we thought were just harmless stories from our grandparents are actually their firsthand accounts of seeing these creatures? With the passing of time, we have grown both closer to our world and further away from it, and so when anything unexplainable comes up, we immediately try to find a reasonable explanation for it instead of just chalking it up to the fairies, as our ancestors would have.

People in recent years are showing both videos and stories about seeing creatures that are very close to descriptions of fairies from the old stories. Some of these tales come to us from Crawfordsville. Several different types of creatures have been seen there, and even fairy circles have been witnessed. Fairy circles, or fairy rings as they are sometimes called, are believed to be doorways between our world and the world of the Fae.

Fairy rings have some interesting lore about them, and they can show up anywhere for any reason. Fairy rings are rings of grass that are different from the other grass around it and usually encircled by something like mushrooms or other things. Mushrooms are the most famous thing that surrounds a fairy ring. These oddball areas in our yards or in the woods look strange to us but also have a scary legend associated with them.

A fairy circle seen in the area. *Photo by authors.*

These rings have been said to be a place where if you step inside, a couple of different things could happen. The most popular is that you will leave our world and find yourself in the world of the fairies. This is a place that changes depending on the story or part of the world you are in. But most of the time, once you have entered the fairy world, you won't be able to get back to the real world.

In rare situations where people have returned, strange things are said to have happened, such as time has passed drastically and in some cases so much time that those you knew have already grown old. This world of the fairy may be a great, wondrous place or a horrible one, but surely it is not somewhere we want to get stuck for the rest of time.

Another thing that is said that could happen is if a person or animal steps into a fairy ring, they get sick or even die. They have disturbed the fairy that controls the ring and so have been made to suffer accordingly. The lucky ones who inadvertently step into a fairy ring are invited to dance the night away with the fairies before returning to their homes in the morning. Fairy rings have been sighted all around Crawfordsville over the years, which gives more credence to the sightings of fairies that accompany them.

Fairy rings are not the only things to have been spotted in Crawfordsville, however. On a night like any other, a woman was awakened for some unknown reason and decided to get a drink. As she went to get her drink, she flipped the light on and immediately regretted it. Standing in front of the back door looking back at her was something she had never seen before. It was a creature about three to four feet tall, gray skinned, with a bulky build, bald head, no neck and dark black eyes. The lady immediately shut off the light, and when she flipped the switch again, the creature had disappeared. She was so shaken up that when she went back to bed, she wouldn't even speak to her husband at first. After a little while, he was able to get the story out of her, and he began to look up this creature online.

Through doing some research, he found a Trow. Trows are a type of troll that is smaller and sometimes seen around homes. It dwells in small hills or piles of tree limbs and tall grass. They like to be close to homes to take the form of the elderly or young children in hopes people will mistake them for a family member and show them affection.

This got the gentleman thinking about some weird things that had been happening in his home. He had a young daughter, and she would act strange sometimes. Some people said they had seen two of the young girl playing around the house on different days. So even many years later, they tell the story of this Trow creature visiting them and perhaps pretending to be their little girl.

Many people in Crawfordsville tell stories of an often-seen strange sighting, especially in the older parts of the city. People claim to see little people who are very small but perfectly shaped for their size. They are said to range from one to two feet tall and are extremely white—almost pasty white—in color. They have been known to scare children, inviting them to follow them to some unclear destination.

One woman tells how a female would sit on her dresser and she would watch the creature brush her hair. We don't have any stories of them speaking, just watching and beckoning for others to follow them. Several train tracks in the Crawfordsville area go over small creeks, ponds and such. These places seem to have a strangeness to them. Many people go to them and see strange glowing blue figures floating above the water as well as diving down into it.

Strange lights seem to accompany these sightings, and they are well known to happen at night in different parts of the year. When talked about near the older generation of Crawfordsville, all of these strange sightings of fairy circles, Trow, little people and blue figures get you similar stories; they say that when the Irish settled in the area, those fairy creatures accompanied them.

So are these sightings of different types of fairies or something completely different that isn't yet known? It is interesting how often these types of stories are shared and new ones come across in the area of Crawfordsville.

WILLIAM DOYLE'S MONSTER

Throughout history, we have heard stories of people seeing a creature that seems to be either a dinosaur that has survived to our times or a creature that hasn't been discovered before. We have had several strange creature sightings throughout Crawfordsville and the surrounding county, but one that is truly strange is the story of William Doyle. While digging a well on the farm of Braxton Cash, he struck a bed of red stone that collapsed on him. The collapse dragged William deeper underground into some kind of underground passage. William took a moment to collect his thoughts and decided to investigate the chamber. The chamber seemed to extend in a northerly direction from him. It didn't take long before he entered a much larger area and was confronted with a beautiful sight. The chamber was filled with amazing stalactites and running water, and after several minutes of staring around in wonder, he heard a hissing noise.

Out of the darkness came into the view of his candle a creature unlike any he had ever seen. It had the body of a crocodile and the neck of a swan, while the head resembled a large snake. He ran for his life, but the creature followed him back to the place where he had fallen in. He grabbed his pickaxe and swung on the creature, pinning it against the wall to die.

The news of this discovery quickly spread, and a crowd came to investigate. They found the creature still gasping out its last breath. The creature was examined by Professor Coulter of Wabash College, who decided that it must be from the Silurian period. It was then displayed in the city of Crawfordsville for everyone to see.

Crawfordsville Review, *June 14, 1890*

William Doyle has been digging a well on the farm of Major Brax Cash, and on Tuesday he struck a bed of red sandstone, the bottom of which gave way, precipitating him about thirty feet below into a subterranean passage. Mr. Doyle was overcome with fear and wonder, but soon regained his normal equilibrium, and being of a daring nature, determined to explore the cavity, which extended in a northerly direction. Lighting a candle, which he had in his pocket, he started forth, the passage growing larger as he proceeded. He soon found himself in a spacious chamber, and adjusting his candle, he was dazzled by a scene of indescribable beauty. From the ceiling hung stalactic formations of various sizes and of every conceivable form, the points of which, dripping with water, made a brilliant spectacle, appearing like vast constellations of stars in a boundless sky. After feasting his eyes upon this scene of beauty for some time, he made a more minute examination of the room. At the further end he discovered a small body of water, and was on the point of retracing his steps when he heard a loud hissing sound, and, by the light of his candle, was horrified to see a strange gigantic animal swimming rapidly towards him. It had the body of a crocodile, and the neck of a swan, while the head resembled that of a huge snake. Our hero dropped his candle and fled for dear life with the frightful-looking "what-is-it" in hot pursuit. Reaching the spot where he first landed, our hero saw, by the reflected light above, his pick lying near. He picked it up and turned to defend himself. When the hideous beast, with yawning mouth and glistening eyes, was within a few feet of him, he struck it a terrific blow, pinning its head to the wall of the cavern, where it writhed in pain. Just at this juncture the Major's head appeared at the top of the well, and letting a rope down soon had our hero on terra firma. The news of this wonderful subterranean adventure flew like wild fire. A crowd soon collected around the well, and three of the bravest descended. They found the strange animal still pinned to the wall, and gasping in the last of agonies of death. It is now on exhibition in the city. It has been seen by Prof. Coulter, who says it is an animal of the Silurian period, and by some strange freak of nature became confined in its underground prison. The Prof. said it belonged to the family of Aldibrontiphoskiphorniasticos, *or words to the effect.*

PART II

SPIRITUALISM AND THE STRANGE CHARACTERS OF CRAWFORDSVILLE

The Famous Crawfordsville Ghost Club

In cities and towns across the country, you hear stories of people joining secret societies and other groups of like-minded individuals. Here in Crawfordsville, we have several such groups and organizations, but the most interesting, secret and possibly creepy was known across the United States as the Famous Crawfordsville Ghost Club.

The true name of the group was the Society for the Advancement of Belief in Ghosts, and it was created on Halloween night in 1887 by William Ridley, Dr. Henry de Caux and Professor Robert Burton. The purpose of the group was for the sharing of personal stories of encounters with the paranormal, as well as the creation of both a library and museum dedicated to the subject.

The gentlemen hoped to prove the reality of ghosts and the paranormal. Memberships were hard to come by, and the group expanded only rarely, as one must be able to show some kind of proof of having a paranormal experience to join. We know that as of 1891, the group had some twenty members, but little information can be found after that on its membership or happenings.

The building and room where the group met were in themselves eerie, so it is pretty obvious why the members chose them. The windows of the building on the north side overlook the Oak Hill Cemetery, while those on the west side look directly down into the jail yard where several hangings happened. The room where they met was called the Ghost Lodge, a dance hall where a man had been murdered some years before. The ghost of the slain young man was said to revisit the scene often. Several other deaths had occurred in the building as well. A painter had fallen from the scaffold of the building to his death, and an elderly woman had dropped dead from a heart issue while searching for her son in the gambling hall.

The hall was decorated to increase the spooky feeling of the members and visitors to it. The hall was hung entirely in white cheesecloth drapes from the walls to the ceiling. White canvas covered the floor, and the windowpanes were painted white as well. Most of the furniture and objects in the hall were black as midnight except certain things, such as the skeletons that stood in each corner of the hall with their craniums turned toward a red glass chimney. These skeletons gave off the only light in the room during meetings, and the light from the makeshift lanterns glowed through their empty eye sockets and grinning mouths. The table where the president and secretary of the group sat was an old dissecting table from the Indiana Medical College. The president called the meetings to order with a large dinner bell that hung from the ceiling above. The bell was from a farmhouse where an infant had died, and the rope that rang it was none other than the rope that was used to hang Jack Henning. The seats of the room were all made from the timbers of the scaffolding where Henning and others were hanged. The library had hundreds of books about ghosts and ghost life, and there was a museum with many ghastly relics.

The members of the group read papers during the meetings detailing their experiences with ghosts, and many of these stories were published in newspapers across the United States. Two such stories follow:

Sacramento Daily Union, *October 31, 1891*
"The Ghost of My Client"
Several years ago Buck Stout was hanged at Rockville, Ind., after taking a change of venue from Montgomery County. His victim was a huckster named Dunbar, whom Buck, having enticed to a lonely place in the woods, killed and robbed. Although arrested at once for the crime, none of the stolen money was found upon the murderer, who died stoutly protesting his innocence. Soon after the execution his old neighbors near Darlington began to complain of the visits of the ghost of this deceased gentleman. In this connection Buck's attorney, Colonel John R. Courtney, read some time since, the following paper before the Crawfordsville Ghost Club:

"It was not long after my handsome client Buck Stout had been hanged that reports began to come to me from Darlington to the effect that his ghost was promenading around that section of country terrifying the women, and

even causing the marrow of Darlington's brave men to turn a trifle cool. Knowing that my client had died a guilty man, with a terrible falsehood upon his lips, I was not at all surprised to hear of his spirit's perambulations, but I candidly confess that I was surprised at the visit which that spirit paid me and at the results of it as well. I was busied with my practice, and paid but little attention to the ghost talk until one night, about three months after the rumor became current, when the matter was brought home to me in a most forcible manner. 'Twas in October and after a hard day's work I had retired to my rooms, very tired, nervous and about half sick. I retired early, but although much fatigued was unable to fall asleep. Hearing the old church clock strike the weary hours I tossed and tumbled about on my couch until after 11 o'clock, when I fell into an uneasy slumber. I judge that I could not have slept over a few minutes when suddenly I found myself wide awake and sitting up in bed trembling as with a chill. In accents all too familiar, spoken as from a far-off planet, but terribly distinct, I had heard my name called.

THE MESSAGE

"Breathlessly I listened for a repetition of that plaintive, wailing cry, and it came. From whence I could not tell—from all around me, from an infinite distance, from nowhere—but it came, and the following words rang through my soul rather than through my ears: 'John! John! For the good Lord's sake, come to the office! Come down at once!'

"There was no mistaking that voice. It was that of my unfortunate client, Stout, but wonderfully sepulchral and subdued. As in a dream, obeying an influence I could not, neither cared to, control, I arose, and having dressed, passed silently out into the night. A death-like stillness hung over the deserted streets and the pavements were weird and startling. I hesitated at the foot of the stairway which led to my office, but, shaking off my fear, I climbed the steps, and, unlocking the door, pushed it wide open. Curiously I gazed into the dark interior. I saw nothing, but gradually became sensitive of another presence than mine. Again on the threshold I hesitated, but taking heart as before, I marched boldly in and closed the door behind me. I had crossed the room and was about raising a window when the old voice, still far off it seemed, exclaimed:

"'John, don't you know me?'

"I quickly wheeled, and standing, not six feet away, I beheld the ghost of my client. There was no doubt about its being only his ghost, for I had seen the sturdy Buck meet a fearful death, and had afterward seen his cold and silent corpse packed safely away under six feet of clay. And then it was a

good, old-fashioned, honest ghost I saw before me, pale, shadowy and woe-be gone, silently awaiting my response, with its ethereal legs sadly mixed up in the waste basket.

"'Buck,' said I (I fear my voice was somewhat shaky), 'how are you?'

"'I'm in torment,' replied the ghost, as it passed its airy hand over its airy brow as though to wipe away immaterial perspiration. 'I died with a secret, and I'm in torment. I come now to you for aid, and I want you to do me a last favor.'

"'Buck,' I returned, 'when I took your case I said that I would stand by you to the end. I thought the end was over months ago, but a lawyer should always be loyal to a client; so name your request and I will grant it.'

A GRATIFIED SPOOK

"That ghost gave a positive sigh of relief, and its countenance lighted up as you have sometimes seen the moonlight up the fleece-like clouds after emerging from a thunder bank.

"'John,' it whispered, 'your last service is by far your greatest, as you will in future learn. I want you to act in behalf of justice now. I want to make partial restitution to poor Dunbar's widow. When I shot him out there in the woods (here the ghost shuddered like steam vapor blown by the wind) I buried his money on the south side of that oak stump near which they found him. I left $337 there, and I want you to get it for his family. Then maybe I can rest. Promise me now to do it, John,' and the whisper died wearily away.

"Of course I promised, and now being quite at my ease with my translated client, or rather with the translated spirit of my late client, I undertook some little research into the question of spiritual entity.

"'Buck,' queried I, after a painful pause in which my caller seemed preparing itself for departure, 'how is it where you are? Do they treat you well?'

"The ghost actually squirmed, and fidgeting with an imaginary button on its imaginary vest, asked in evident embarrassment the time. I quickly called the hour, and before my guest could bid me farewell I had again launched into the subject of escatology [sic] by inquiring:

"'Now, old fellow, what is the use in your trying to dodge the point at issue? What's the climate of your present abode? Come, say.'

"I was aware of the fact that Buck had been a great admirer of the 'myriad-minded bard' during his imprisonment, but was wholly unprepared to hear his ghost declaim in piping, far-off accents:

"'But that I am forbid to tell the secrets of my prison house,
I could a tale unfold whose lightest word
Would harrow up thy soul; freeze thy young blood,
Make thy two eyes like stars start from their spheres;
Thy knotted and combined locks to part
And each particular hair to stand on end
Like quills upon the fretful porcupine;
But this eternal blazon must not be
To ears of flesh and blood.'

"No sooner was the last word uttered than my visitor, who had been growing more and more shadowy throughout his speech, disappeared, and leaving my office in its wanted gloom. So suddenly, however, did a realization of the ghost's departure come upon me that I lost no time in vacating the room, and was conscious of stumbling over the waste-basket and several chairs in making my exit.

THE MONEY FOUND

"How I got home and to bed I cannot recall, but next remember my awakening the following morning with a splitting headache and a perfect recollection of my late experience with a spook. Although, as I say, my recollection in regard to my midnight visitor was extremely vivid, nevertheless, I was more than half inclined to doubt it, and by the time I had disposed of my breakfast I was almost ready to believe that I had been the victim of a nightmare, grim and horrible. I was to be undeceived, however, for on reaching my office I found the door wide open as I had left it in my flight the night before. Three chairs were upset and the contents of the waste-basket strewn recklessly over the floor. I dropped helplessly into a chair and sat there for half an hour, when I arose and proceeded to a livery stable. In three hours more I had visited the scene of the murder and found buried in a small wooden box at the side of the oak stump, the $337 of blood money. I lost no time in tendering this sum to Dunbar's family, and advised them to keep quiet in regard to the matter. This they certainly did and my experience ended with the restitution.

"The ghost of my client is the only ghost I ever saw, but for all that I believed in ghosts before I ever heard of Buck or his ghost either, for the uneasy spirit of my own great-grandfather once walked among the ruins of his old manor house in Ireland, armed with the very pistol he grasped when killed in a duel of his own provoking. My great-grand-father had been a hard man, and half the booby Squires in the county took a shot at his ghost

with their blunderbusses during his moonlight strolls about his old home. None of them ever seemed to discommode him, but every mother's son of them met with some misfortune soon after encroaching on his solitude, and I have no doubt that their ills were visited upon them by the spirit they had wantonly insulted. It is always best to be deferential to a ghost."

The second story is as follows:

THE HAUNTED MILL

A few miles from the sleepy village of Yountsville stands a large, rambling old structure, known in the country round about as the "Hibernian Mill." Over a mile from any public road, the only approach to it is along a grass-grown, deserted lane; and, looming up as the mill does—moss-covered and desolate, a frowning bluff in its rear and the forest on every side—it is not strange that the very surroundings should give rise to tales of the weird and supernatural.

Many years ago the creek which furnished the mill with its power changed its bed, and where once a roaring torrent dashed down the ravine a tiny spring-fed brooklet now winds dreamily through the dark shadows to the river. The change in the creek's bed rendered the mill worthless, thus ruining its owner, who suddenly disappeared soon after his misfortune. What became of him was never known until two years ago, and how the mystery of his disappearance was finally solved is told by James R. Hanna in the following paper recently read before the club:

THE MILL AND THE MILLER

"It was in the summer of 1887 that a party of college friends and myself went into camp at Indian Ford a few miles above Yountsville, in the vicinity of the Hibernian Mill. The hunting and fishing were excellent, and as for the solitude, there was a superabundance of it. The old mill was the only building in a radius of two miles, and that was so covered with Virginia creeper and other tangled vines that it resembled a great bank of fiery blossoms and bright leaves rather than the handiwork of man. Before coming I had heard much of the ghost of the old miller Garineau that walked of nights, and was held in such respect by the county folk that they would not come within half a mile of the mill to gather berries or search for straying cattle. The mill had been built in an outlandishly wild place in order to obtain advantage of a splendid fall and other natural aids to the milling business. When the great freshet of 1868 threw the bed of his creek

four miles away Garineau, who was dependent solely upon the mill, was practically reduced to pauperism. A childless widower, he had lived for years reticent and solitary, but after his misfortune he became sullen and morose, never stirring from his windmill. A few farmers called on him occasionally, and found him either sitting on the mounting-block in front with his face buried in his hands, or wandering aimlessly through the great building, which, though worthless now, had cost him a small fortune. His visitors became less numerous and his moroseness greater. He would converse with no one, and finally two speculators who came to purchase his machinery could find him nowhere. His room contained all his effects, but he was gone as from the world. Years passed and the property was sold for taxes. A part of the machinery and the mill-stones were removed, but the old structure was allowed to stand, a melancholy monument to the uncertainty of human aims and expectations.

GARINEAU'S GHOST

"Yet though the mill stood there so silently, it was rumored about in time that the ghost of old Garineau held high carnival in the lonesome rooms. Sturdy schoolboys, who passed their days playing truant in the woods, came whimpering home at dusk with wild tales of having seen an apparition at the mill. Squirrel hunters saw 'the haunt' as they quietly crept up the old creek bed peering about for game, and they usually lost no time in giving it a wide berth. Uncle Jimmy Dawson, the veteran coon hunter, was out with his hounds one night and treed a coon in a small buckeye just behind the mill. Now, Uncle Jimmy wasn't afraid of 'haunts,' not he, and was swinging his ax, with a right good will, when suddenly his eager hounds dropped their tails, and, uttering low whines, sulked rapidly off into the brush. Uncle Jimmy, looking up from his work to see what caused all this, saw what made even his stout heart quail, and giving vent to a squall of terrified dismay, he fled precipitately from the spot. Looking from the window of the mill loft was the ghost itself, frowning angrily down upon him, and attired, as Uncle Jimmy ever afterward maintained, in the same red cloak that old Garineau wore many years before when the mill was opened at the time of the grand barbecue given in its honor by the countryside. In view of all these experiences, then, it is not strange that the simple and superstitious people of that section soon learned to shun the wild dell at whose mouth the haunted mill stood like a sentinel guard. With the spirit of romance and bravado, so incident to youth, the members of our camping party delighted to hunt up and down the ghost-ridden glen, declaring that we would shoot the spook on

sight. We kicked open the rotten door of the old mill and sacrilegiously joked and declaimed in the gloomy, cobwebbed rooms, which for years had known no earthly visitants. We ascended into the great storeroom above, and in the gloom and confusion one of the boys came near falling through a black hole in the center of the floor. This hole was the opening to sort of a chute into which grain had once been poured to conduct it to the hopper. Over two feet at the opening, it gradually narrowed until at the hopper this funnel was but six inches in diameter. The hole was then filled with dust and cobwebs, and would have been anything but a pleasant place into which to have fallen. We explored the garret or loft, and looked down from the window upon the very buckeye tree at which Jimmy Dawson was hacking away when interrupted by the ghost. We sang and hallooed through the old shell in a most demonstrative manner, and if our spook was anywhere in hearing it must have been mortally offended.

AN EVENTFUL EXPEDITION

"We had been in camp for probably ten days, when late one afternoon it was discovered that some of our supplies were entirely out. It fell to me, after some parley, to ride six miles to Yountsville and stock up. Hunting our horse in the pasture required some time, and when I passed the old mill, on my way to the village, it was almost nightfall, and when I finally reached the pike, after a hard ride down the desert lane, it was dark. It was after 9 o'clock when I left Yountsville for my return to camp, and in the west the clouds hung black and glowering, obscuring the moon which had lighted me on my way. Long before I reached the lane, over whose rough and broken way I dreaded to ride in total darkness, the heavens were reverberating with the echoes of the thunder which heralded the approach of a beating storm. I cursed my bad luck most heartily, and reaching the lane I lashed my horse along the perilous route at the imminent risk of breaking both our necks. The occasional flashes of lightning kept me keenly alive to a sense of my danger by revealing the stones, washouts and gullies in the path, but, intent on reaching the sheltering mill before the rain poured down, I urged my panting beast forward. We were about a hundred yards from the old building when the first large drops began to patter on the parched, gasping earth, and I had barely time to lead my willing horse through the wide door, which we had kicked open a few days before, when down came the rain. A puff of wind, accompanied by a dash of rain, a momentary, death-like lull, a crash of thunder and the storm was on. The building swayed with the violence of the wind, and through the numerous large cracks the water

51

came dashing in, wetting me to the skin. I recollected that the wareroom was boarded on the inside for protection from the dampness, and lost no time in running up the rickety stairway to this dry retreat, over twenty feet above. It seemed warm and inviting, and, throwing my saddlebags in a corner, I sat down upon them, resolved to wait until the storm had passed over before I started for our camp, which was a mile away, down a rough and brush-grown creek bank. Gradually the fury of the storm spent itself, but as the rain continued to descend in torrents, I determined to spend the night where I was, and, closing my eyes, I soon was fast asleep.

THE GHOST

"It must have been almost midnight when I was awakened by hearing my horse in the room below give a terrified scream which sounded almost human. Before I was fairly awake I heard him tearing from the mill-room out into the night. The rain had ceased to fall, and the last beams of the declining moon lighted up the large room through its one great window with an unearthly glow. Startled by the commotion made by my horse, I sat up in my corner, and was in the act of raising my hands to rub my eyes when I fell back in a helpless heap, for coming up the stairway from below I saw the ghost!

"An old man with a set and care-worn face, a fierce, hunted light shining in the eyes, which seemed to see nothing, a trembling hand which drew tightly around his slight, bent form a bright scarlet cloak—that was the ghost. Overpowered with conflicting emotions I sat breathlessly watching my strange companion from another sphere. He saw me not, but, murmuring and gibbering to himself, began to pace the room. I could not distinguish all his speech, but 'ruin! ruin! ruin!' was the burden of the self-communion. At first he passed quite close to me as he walked about the musty wareroom, but gradually his circle became smaller and smaller as he neared the center. Finally he paused almost at the edge of the chute and groaned. I was gazing intently at him, when suddenly he took a forward step, and like a flash shot down the chute with a shriek, which still is ringing in my ears. This cry broke the spell which bound me, and leaping to my feet I rushed down the stairs and fled out through the bushes, which were dripping with the water, and which cut and chilled me as I brushed them hurriedly aside. I paused not until I reached our camp, and fell almost fainting among my companions, who had been awakened by the arrival of my horse some time before, and who were just preparing to set out in search of me.

THE INVESTIGATION

"*I was too greatly excited and fatigued to give a coherent account of my adventures that night, but the following morning, after a good breakfast and a drink of brandy, I managed to tell my story. So real was it all to me that the shouts of laughter with which my companions received it filled me with surprise, anger and disgust. Hot words were followed by mutual apologies, and after a good deal of persuasion I was induced to return to the mill with two of my friends, Binford and Fox, in quest of the supplies which I had left there the night before. I was still angry, and it annoyed me not a little to be conscious of the tact that my companions were silently chuckling at my expense. Binford, in his loud, bluff way, insisted upon relating the exceedingly flat story of 'Harry and the Guide Post,' while Fox graciously condescended to repeat a short poem which treated of a ghost which proved to be a frog. Fairly choking with choler I arrived at the mill and proceeded with my friends up into the wareroom to get the saddle-bags. I had picked them up and was turning away again when I heard Binford exclaim, 'What's this?' and looking quickly to where he stood in the center of the room, I saw him holding up what caused beads of perspiration to stand out upon my forehead and my limbs to shake with terror, He held in his hand a large scarlet cloak, the identical garment, it seemed, the ghost had worn the night before, the same pattern, the same shade. I almost looked to see it vanish into thin air: but no, it was good, stout material. For a moment the terrible thought struck me that perhaps I had been the witness of a real catastrophe that perhaps a fellow-being had fallen into the chute before my eyes and perished. A glance into the hole, however, undeceived me. Those cobwebs had not been disturbed for years.*

"'*This is the same cloak your ghost wore, Hanna,' exclaimed Binford with a jarring laugh. 'The old fellow was probably just retiring for the night when you saw him, and as his cloak is here yet, he's probably still in bed. If so we'll roust him out.'*

"*Stepping to the side of the room he tore off a long weather strip which was fastened over a crack and returning threw it into the funnel with a loud halloo. Instead of shooting through to the hopper, as we expected, it met with some impediment about half way down and stopped there, the end still protruding into the wareroom. Binford seized the pole and began to prod the obstruction vigorously, calling out that he had the ghost cornered now and would finish him forever. A great fear began to take possession of my soul.*

"'It's a bag of wheat which has fallen down and stuck there,' Binford finally exclaimed. 'But it feels queer, too,' he added as he gave it another poke. 'Must to satisfy myself I'm going down below and split the old chute open to see what's in it.'

THE MILLER'S FATE

"Curiously we followed him, and in my heart I felt what the result of that search would be. Climbing upon the hopper Binford thrust an old crowbar between the decaying boards of which the chute was made, and with a mighty wrench tore one of them off. Both my companions gave a cry of horror at the spectacle revealed, but I, expecting such a sight, stood by almost unmoved. There, wedged tightly in the grain chute of his own mill, was the distorted and mummified body of old miller Garineau. The flesh and skin had dried like parchment, but still the ghastly yellow face exhibited traces of the unutterable agony in which the poor wretch had died. No need to explain the manner of his death. I had seen a spiritual repetition of the tragedy the night before, and my companions stared alternately at me, the scarlet cloak and the withered corpse with superstitious horror. We said but little, and since that day my friends have shunned the discussion of our dread discovery. The following day the campers and several neighbors laid the body of old Garineau to rest in a country graveyard several miles away, wrapping him in the same scarlet cloak which had led to the discovery of his remains. Since then the ghost has never once been seen, although the place is still shunned by the country folk, my experience rather increasing the feeling of superstition with which it is regarded. I have never solved the mystery of the scarlet cloak. I know it was not there the day we first explored the mill, and all the old inhabitants stated that it was undoubtedly the garment of the unfortunate miller. I can swear I saw the ghost attired in it, but that is all. It is to me forever a part of the great mystery which unites the natural with the supernatural, the material with the immaterial."

—J.A. Greene, *Crawfordsville, Indiana, correspondent of the* St. Louis Globe-Democrat

What happened to the group after 1891 hasn't been found, but maybe somewhere in the town people still meet and the group still exists, hidden from public view.

SPIRITUALISM

In the nineteenth century, Spiritualism was on the rise. What began as a simple movement with the belief in life after death soon turned into a full-fledged religion, touting powers of healing and communication with the deceased. As the borders between science and religion began to blur, Spiritualism found its place in many minds and hearts and began to take off across the United States. The real beginnings of the movement started with the infamous Fox sisters. The sisters made a name for themselves through their claims that they could commune with the dead through a series of rapping noises that the spirits would produce during séances in answer to their questions. For years, the sisters traveled throughout the United States, showing off their gifts and dazzling many people, but after one of the sisters came forward admitting it had all been a sham, it ended for them. Margaret Fox admitted that she and her sister would make the rapping noises with their toes and even traveled again through the states to show people how they had fooled everyone. This, however, did nothing to slow the rise of other mediums and spirit communicators.

Séances were not the only kind of spiritualism people gathered around. Spiritual healing was also in full swing. People would crowd lecture halls and travel great distances to see, heal and receive healing from magicians and witch doctors. These spiritual doctors would claim they could heal any number of ailments, including hearing loss, cataracts, liver disease, rheumatoid arthritis, paralysis, tumors and more. They would perform their miracles in front of crowds for all to see how powerful and curative they really were. It was a grand show, and many people of the time put their lives in the hands of these doctors.

Ghost photography was also a widely popular attraction during this time. People would sit to have their pictures taken, anxiously excited to see if a deceased loved one or friend would appear with them. Disembodied heads or ethereal bodies would show up, to the delight or horror of the participant. Some photographs would show one spirit, and others would have several. This phenomenon was rampant throughout the world and caught the attention of many famous people.

In the late 1800s and early 1900s, Crawfordsville was a hub of spiritualist activities. Leaders of the movement would often visit to lecture and give séances here in the downtown hotels, including Eva Fay, the famous psychic and high priestess of mysticism, who visited on several occasions. They were widely respected and renowned and often would speak to crowds as large as fifty. However, Crawfordsville had its very own soothsayers, witch doctors, mediums, fortunetellers, ghost photographers and spooks, many of whom were well-respected leaders of the town and county. There was a Church of Spiritualism in town, and mediums were trained and taught how to perform circles to commune with the other side.

The local papers would often write articles about the visiting spiritualists and other activities going on in the county concerning the mystical and the other side. The local churches held lectures and debates to inform the congregations about Spiritualism and its link to Christianity. There were street corner lecturers out to herd the masses into Spiritualism. During the height of the movement and even after its eventual downward slope throughout the rest of the United States, Crawfordsville was all in and thriving on Spiritualism.

A.D. Willis and Spirit Photography

The beginnings of spirit photography—not to be confused with the more modern ghost photography—come to us from the 1850s. In 1856, Sir David Brewster realized that using different effects could cause long exposure on pictures, making them look as though they had a ghostly visitor during a photography sitting. This was taken a step forward when such double-exposed photos were put on display at a showing for the London Stereoscopic Company called "The Ghost in the Stereoscope."

Soon after and into the 1920s, people began seeing more and more of these photos as the number of people who owned cameras grew. There were many defenders of the photos, such as Sir Arthur Conan Doyle, and just as many against them, such as Harry Houdini and P.T. Barnum. An American by the name of William H. Mumler is probably one of the most famous spirit photographers of the time. He was proven to be a fraud and brought up on charges for it. The most famous Mumler spirit photograph is a photograph that First Lady Mary Todd Lincoln posed for with what was said to be her assassinated husband, President Abraham Lincoln.

In 1869, Mumler was arrested for fraud when it was found that one of his "spirits" was a living, breathing person. He was acquitted in court despite the evidence against him. Many were convinced that spirit photography was real, and a few frauds couldn't sway their beliefs in the phenomenon. Several books were written about the subject. Some, like "The Case for Spirit Photography," written by Arthur Conan Doyle, were in favor, and

Left: William and Bessie May Woodworth. *Courtesy of Lucinda Brooks*.

Right: Benjamin and Dollie Clark. *Courtesy of Lucinda Brooks*.

others, like "The Table-Rappers" by Ronald Pearsall, were against. Some other well-known individuals in the field were David Duguid and Edward Wyllie, who were also later found to be frauds.

In December 1869, Crawfordsville joined the spirit photography phenomenon. A local man by the name of Abner Denham Willis began claiming that he was being haunted. Willis told the local paper that it started with occasional unsolicited appearances of ghostly images on his negatives. He went on to say that many called him a soul sleeper. He was horrified with these unaccountable manifestations and tried to rid his place of business of any sign of them. When people came to him asking for spirit photos to be taken of them, he refused and would ask them to immediately leave his place of business.

Fisher Doherty and other spiritualists consoled him with the thought that perhaps he was a spiritual medium. He refused this notion though and sought out the counsel of his pastor, the Reverend Hatch, who told him that the gallery must be under the control of demons. After several unbelievers recognized individuals in his photos, Willis began to reconcile to the theory that he was a spiritual medium.

What set Abner Willis apart from others of his time was that even after many in-depth investigations by people with the knowledge to see anything done purposely to create the ghosts in the photos, he was never found to be false, fake or in any way ungenuine in his dealings with people. Fisher Doherty even placed a reward for anyone who could prove Willis to be faking the phenomenon. It was never paid out.

Crawfordsville Review, *January 8, 1870*
Spiritual Photography
Mr. Fisher Doherty:—Dear Sir: In reply to your request that I furnish you a statement of the result of my investigation of Spirit Photography in the rooms of Mr. Willis, of Crawfordsville, I have to say that having business in Montgomery county, Ind., and hearing while there that Mr. Willis was taking spirit pictures, I visited his rooms for the purpose of investigating. Introducing myself to Mr. Willis as an artist, he invited me to examine his room, camera, plates, &., which I did carefully, satisfying myself that there was nothing more than what is ordinarily used in the process of photography.

While in the room a man by the name of Pefley, from Tippecanoe County, Ind., came in and asked to have a spirit picture. Willis seated him and asked me to focus the instrument which I did. Mr. Willis then took a new ferrotype plate from the box and flowed it with collodion. We together entered the dark room and put the plate in the bath, from the bath to the box, and from there to the camera room. I again examined the camera and found it all right. I placed the cap on the tube. Mr. Willis removed the cap—my position was directly behind the instrument, so that I could observe the operator, the subject and the instrument at the same moment; the operator's back was turned to the subject, one hand rested lightly on the instrument. Went with him to the dark room saw the plate taken from the box and lost sight of it during the developing process. Then appeared on the plate a picture of the setter, and in the distance that of a little girl, apparently about five years old and well defined. Mr. Pefley pronounced it to be that of a little daughter deceased about five years. A brother of Mr. Pefley also pronounced it to a daughter of the latter. There was no one beside or near Mr. Pefley while sitting. Throughout there

Spirit photograph taken by Abner Willis. *Courtesy of Beverly Wilgus.*

*was nothing deficient in the manifestation from that usually practiced in
photography. Nothing of fraud or deception that I could discern. Cannot
account for the spirit picture.*
Respectfully
J.W. Byrkett

Willis would go so far as to use another photographer's studio and
supplies under careful supervision, and the images would still appear.
There is even a story that his being in the general area caused other
photographers to have spirits show up in their work, to the amazement of
the photographers involved.

Willis's popularity grew, and his photos ended up in galleries in
Indianapolis, Chicago and other cities across the Midwest. With his death in
1898, he went to his rest remaining a photographer who was believed to be
a genuine spirit medium. It was never proven that he faked his photos.

Fisher Doherty

During the 1800s, there lived in Crawfordsville an interesting man. This man was one of the most prominent citizens of this city. He was famous all across the state and was even considered a candidate for governor. He was a member of the Underground Railroad, and most slaves who came through this area on their way to Canada stayed at his home, which was located on the corner of Green and Pike Streets. He was an inventor and held a patent with his partner, E.L. Sies, for a two-wheeled vehicle. He was a businessman and owned a prominent carriage business with his sons. His name was Fisher Doherty, and he also believed himself to be a medium and a spirit photographer.

While this man helped hundreds of people during his time, he was considered a little different. He was a huge believer in Spiritualism and the belief in the spirit world. He was known to be friends with most of the people in the area who practiced Spiritualism, mediumship, spirit photography and so on. There were also claims that he bewitched people and placed spirits within them, that he was an agent for the devil and that he came from hell, but all who knew him personally thought him to be of great character and respected and admired him.

Doherty spent much of his time—when he wasn't helping slaves—touring and talking about Spiritualism. He was a great believer in spirit photography and insisted on all his friends sitting for photos. He put up a great sum of money for anyone who could prove his friend A.D. Willis, the famous spirit photographer, a fraud, but luckily for him, that never came about. When

The Doherty grave marker at Old Oak Hill Cemetery. *Photo by authors.*

Fisher Doherty's grave marker at Old Oak Hill Cemetery. *Photo by authors.*

Doherty himself began taking spirit photographs, he also put up $5,000 to anyone who could prove him a fraud. He had a great collection of photographs and loved showing them off.

> Crawfordsville Weekly Journal, *October 14, 1869*
> *Among the curiosities at the Fair were Fisher Doherty's spirit photographs, taken by Willis. They were probably the first of the kind ever exhibited at an agricultural fair, and were the objects of much wonder and speculation among the dubious.*

Doherty created a place in Crawfordsville that he called the Spiritual Hall. It was on Washington Street over Darter's Produce Store and was a place for people to learn about Spiritualism as well as experience the wonders performed by the mediums, fortunetellers and magicians who visited the area. Fisher Doherty was one of the leaders of Spiritualism in Crawfordsville and did more than anyone to promote its success, often by giving street corner lectures on the subject to any who would listen. He would host Halloween parties and séances in his home, often inviting mediums from across the state to stay with him and entertain his guests.

> Crawfordsville Review, *February 11, 1871*
> *Spiritual Hall—This Elegant hall, devoted to the mysteries of the unseen world, has at last been formally opened under the auspices of Mr. Fisher Doherty, the great shining light and apostle of Spiritualism. For the last twenty years Mr. D. has been an ardent and zealous advocate and teacher of the sublime truths of man's immortality as proved by the evidence of spiritual communication with those who once inhabited our earth. Not withstanding persecution and ridicule, he has never swerved from what he considered his duty in imparting to his fellow men a more thorough and practical knowledge of the "summer land" than could be gained from the pulpits of our fashionable churches. Spiritual Hall, we understand, is to be one of the fixed institutions of our city; a reporter for the weary pilgrim who would learn something of the geography and climatic condition of a land to which he must sooner or later emigrate. The Hall is located on Washington Street, over Darter's Produce Store. It is furnished in a neat and plain style. The walls are decorated with spiritual scenes and portraits of eminent spiritualists. A fine photograph instrument is kept in the hall, and we learn that spirit pictures are frequently taken. A cabinet will soon be put up when some very astonishing manifestations will take place, at least such is the*

*promise made by Mr. D. by the spirits. The number of spiritualists in our
city is rapidly increasing, and embraces among its believers many of our
most respectable and wealthy citizens.*

With all the mysteriousness of Spiritualism, spirit photography and being
a supposed medium around him, Doherty continued to be one of the most
respected citizens Crawfordsville ever knew. He was praised and respected
all the way until the day of his death at age seventy-three. His funeral was
said to be the largest Crawfordsville had ever seen, with hundreds of people
flowing in and out of the house, the sidewalks and the road. Even after his
death, however, he was not through with promoting Spiritualism. His ghost
was said to commune regularly with his friends and give advice but refused
to tell them about the other side and how things were there.

THE WITCH OF ATHENS: MADAME CROW

In the midst of the Spiritualism movement, there were many people who came to make claims, cash in and speak up on behalf of the other side. While Spiritualism was on a downward turn in the country, it was still thriving in Crawfordsville. There was no shortage of travelers from around the state to provide these entertainments for the citizens, but Crawfordsville had its very own talent in the form of Mary Love Crowe, better known throughout the county as Madame Crowe. At that time, many fortunetellers adopted the title of "Madame" in a professional setting.

In this period of history, fortunetellers were not sought out by good, upstanding people. They ran establishments to be visited under the cover of night and in secret. Madame Crowe, however, was often featured in the papers around town, her patrons gladly sharing their experiences with reporters and friends.

Madame Crowe was both respected and ridiculed for her talents. People flocked to her establishment in Ladoga and her home in Crawfordsville, down in the Goose Nibble, from all across the state to get their cards read, find lost items, hear the names of their future spouses, help find cures for illnesses, find lost animals and more. She was a known eccentric, keeping shop in the back of a mortuary and using a coffin as a bench. She would go into trances in which she would writhe and chant in ominous tones. People made wild claims about her, such as that she drank blood, spit fire, had human skeletons in her home and kept company with black cats, but that did not stop them from dropping their coins into her coffers to ask their questions.

While she had a few very public and infamous blunders in her predictions—one of which nearly cost another person his life when an angry mob set out to hang him for the murder of a child that was later found very much alive—she was also known to get a lot of things right. She accurately predicted the outcome of Congressman Vory Brookshire's campaign when he came to seek her counsel. He even told of his unfortunate loss and her accurate prediction of it in front of Congress in Washington.

Madame Crowe was married three times and had four children during her lifetime. She died in December 1894 after a long illness with pneumonia, at the age of seventy-four. The town expected something spectacularly paranormal to come about with her passing, but it was a quiet event, and she was buried in Oak Hill Cemetery after a funeral was held in her home. Even after her death, people wrote to the town seeking her advice, not knowing she had passed.

DR. WILLIAM DE CAUX TILNEY

Throughout the history of Crawfordsville, we find lots of doctors. Some are even pretty famous, but one of the most interesting had to be Dr. William De Caux Tilney. This man truly believed he was more than a doctor; he thought he was a magician and he could cure anything in men and women with what he called "eclectic medicines." He was born in England in 1841 before coming to the United States in 1867. He married in Crawfordsville in 1871 and resided in the town for the rest of his life.

He was a typical Englishman of the time, the papers said. He was fat, genial and jolly. He was a decided prohibitionist, abstaining from all alcoholic drinks. During his service in the English navy, he was known to toss his drink ration over the side of the ship rather than imbibe alcohol. Dr. Tilney studied medicine at the Pennsylvania State University, Milton S. Hershey Medical Center and the Philadelphia University of Medicine and Surgery. He had a local practice in Crawfordsville but also traveled around the country doing tours where he promised to cure any and all ailments. His path of study was as an allopath, which is a doctor who treats a person's symptoms and diseases with medicines and surgeries.

Dr. Tilney was most famous for his touring and curing of those who were thought to be incurable with his "wondrous powers of healing" in just about twenty to thirty minutes. Dr. Tilney even promised that he would examine people for free and charge nothing unless he could cure them. He would perform surgeries and procedures on people in front of audiences and leave them astounded when those who previously couldn't hear were able to hear a

Dr. Tilney's grave marker at Old Oak Hill Cemetery. *Photo by authors.*

whisper and those who couldn't walk into the lecture hall walked out on their own. He was known to break the crutches of those he cured to demonstrate their lack of need for them when he was done. Doctors and ministers alike would come to see him talk and do his miracles. Dr. Tilney successfully cured hundreds of people, and the very thankful patients would write to the local papers exclaiming their joy for his work and endorsing him to others.

However, Dr. Tilney was arrested and charged with the death of Edward Skinner of Grand Junction, Colorado, in March 1900. The charges were brought after Skinner visited Dr. Tilney's lecture and took his cure-all medicine. Later that same night, he passed away, and his wife immediately contacted the local police, placing all blame on Dr. Tilney and his medicines.

Dr. Tilney proclaimed his innocence, saying that he was the victim of trumped-up charges by doctors who were jealous of his healing powers. After a trial, Dr. Tilney was found innocent of all wrongdoing, as the state chemist claimed the medicine he had given wouldn't hurt a mouse. Tilney went through all his life claiming his wondrous powers and his true belief in Spiritualism. He died at his home in Crawfordsville of a stroke in 1925.

JOHN COFFEE

Like many towns across the country, Crawfordsville has seldom had any major crimes. A little of this and that, but when something as major as a murder happens, it rocks the entire town. From history, very few murderers met their last moments here in Crawfordsville, but one of the most famous of those who did was the case of John Coffee (not to be confused with the character from Stephen King's book with the same name).

In January 1885, the state was shaken with the news of the bodies of James and Elizabeth McMullen being pulled from the burned remains of their home near Elmdale, Indiana. John Coffee, twenty-three, was quickly arrested for the crime while wearing the clothes of the victims.

John Coffee was the son of a widow and was raised by Frank Bagley, who happened to live near the McMullens. John had never been in trouble, and many said he was slow in the head. There were many in the area who didn't believe that John was the person behind the deaths. After being arrested, John escaped but was quickly caught once again.

When John was questioned, he gave different accountings of what happened, but each time he did admit to being at the home during the killings. In one interview, he claimed to have committed the killings; in another, he claimed it was done by someone else while he looked on; and yet on a third time, he claimed once again to have just watched as it was done. This caused many to question what really happened and for another man, James Dennis, to also be arrested for the murders.

JOHN W. C. COFFEE.

A drawing of John Coffee from the newspaper at the time of his hanging. *Courtesy of the Crawfordsville District Public Library.*

In his first interview, John confessed to killing the McMullens over money and described in detail how it was done. He claimed to have visited the home, where he and James sat and talked until Elizabeth left the room. Then he grabbed a stick of wood and struck James, which caused him to fall to the floor, where John hit him again, killing him. Elizabeth opened the door between the rooms, but John quickly grabbed it. He demanded money, but she claimed they only had twenty-five cents in the whole house. John dressed in James's clothes before striking Elizabeth on her head with the stick of wood. He then poured coal oil on her and the bed and set them on fire before leaving to stay at another person's house to spend the night.

About a week after making this confession, he gave a new confession on what had happened that night. He said that he and James Dennis had agreed to steal some chickens, and he had no idea that Dennis had the intention of killing the McMullens. When they arrived at the home, Dennis told Coffee to remain at the gate while he went inside. A few moments passed before Dennis came out of the house, dragging Elizabeth by the hair and demanding Coffee kill her with a stick. He refused, and Dennis hit her himself. They carried her body back into the house before searching it for money and finding some. Dennis dressed Coffee in the clothes of James McMullen before setting fire to the house. As they were heading back, Dennis told Coffee if he was arrested to say that he did it and then Dennis would get him out. Dennis was soon arrested and brought to trial for the murders. He was also convicted for the deaths but had his conviction overturned by the Supreme Court.

Shortly before his time to be hanged for the murders, Coffee made one last confession on what had happened. John told the people that he was invited by James Rankin to the McMullens' for a party. John didn't think this out of the ordinary, as people were always having little parties with friends and family. When he arrived at the house with Rankin, John Curtis and James Dennis, Rankin shot and killed the McMullens. They searched the house for money, and before they left, they set it on fire to cover up the crime. Rankin put his gun to John's head and told him that if he ever told anyone, he would kill him.

John, knowing that he was to die, wanted to clear his conscience before his death and to be forgiven for his part in the horrible crime. The body of James McMullen, when found, had a bullet hole in the head. Rankin was never arrested or tried for these crimes, but Coffee's statement helped to overturn James Dennis's conviction.

Indianapolis Journal, *October 17, 1885*
Coffee's Crime
History of the Murder of James McMullen and Wife, and their Murderer. On the morning of Jan. 8, 1885, about 10 o'clock, the discovery was made by a small neighbor boy that the house of James McMullen, near Elmdale, about nine miles northwest of Crawfordsville, had burned to the ground during the night. The alarm was immediately given, and a crowd was soon on the scene. Water was thrown upon the smoldering ruins, and it was soon discovered that Mr. McMullen and wife had burned. Coroner S.L. Ensminger held an inquest, and it was determined that a murder had been committed, as the body of Mr. McMullen was found among ashes of one room and the remains of his wife were among those of another room. Suspicion was directed toward John W.C. Coffee who was taken in charge by Ben Swank, to be kept until the morning of Jan. 9, when he was to have been examined. That morning, about 6 o'clock, Swank arose and went downstairs, and left Coffee in bed. On his return he found that Coffee had stepped out on a shed roof and jumped to the ground. Thus making his escape. The detective companies were soon in pursuit, and Coffee was arrested on Saturday evening, Jan. 10, by three of their members, Ben Rhoadhamel, Ben Gray and Tom Smith, at the house of Till J. Sloan, near Stringtown, in Fountain County. He was taken back to Elmdale, at which time he made his first confession to the detective company, as follows: "On the evening of Jan. 7, about 7 o'clock, I went to the home of the McMullens, and was admitted by James McMullen. (The home of McMullen was a log-house of two rooms.) McMullen and I sat and talked until Mrs. McMullen went into the other room. Then I picked up a stick of wood and struck McMullen, which caused him to fall to the floor. Then I struck him again. Mrs. McMullen opened the door between the rooms to see what was the trouble, and I forced the door open between the rooms. (Coffee stated that in the scuffle to get the door open, she caught his arm in the door, and he showed the marks on his arm which had been made then.) Then I demanded of Mrs. McMullen to tell me where the money was. She said: 'You should

have come a few days sooner, as we have just paid $60 on a ditch.' We then searched the house, and I found twenty-five cents. Then I put on McMullen's pants and boots. (These he had on when he was among the number who arrived at the scene of the murder on Jan. 8, and still had on when arrested, and was the principal cause of his being suspected.) I then got a pair of her stockings and a spool of thread, and put them in my pocket. Mrs. McMullen proposed then that we go over to James Morrow's and get $20 when he was owing them, and offered to marry me. I refused, and struck her on the head with a stick. I then poured coal oil on her and the feather bed, set them on fire and went to Rankin's, where I slept that night. I could see the house burning while in bed." He stated, also that no one helped him. He was brought to Crawfordsville and put in jail. In about a week he made his second statement. He said that James Dennis proposed to him that they would go and steal some chickens. He agreed to this, but had no idea that Dennis was intending to murder them. When they arrived at McMullen's gate he told Coffee to stay there until he returned. Dennis went to the house, and was admitted. In a short time Coffee heard a noise in the house, and, as he was approaching the door, Dennis came out dragging Mrs. McMullen by the hair, and said, as he handed me a club, "John, you kill her." He said that he could not, and Dennis then took the club and struck her on the head. They then carried her in the house, searched around for money and other articles. Dennis got about $300 and Coffee twenty-five cents. Dennis told Coffee to put on McMullen's pants and boots, which he did. Dennis then put a spool-box in his pocket containing various small articles, after which they set fire to the house and departed. On the way back, Dennis said to Coffee, "if you are arrested, say you did it, and I will see you out." James Dennis was arrested and placed in jail. Coffee's case came up in court on March 30. The jury retired about 4 o'clock P.M., on April 1, and in fifteen minutes returned with a verdict of murder in the first degree. Coffee's lawyers were Paul & Humphries, and the State was represented by Prosecuting Attorney A.B. Anderson and M.A. White. The case of Dennis was called on April 15, and the jury retired on April 21. In four hours they brought in a verdict of murder in the first degree. The lawyers for the State were the same as in Coffee's trial, and Dennis was defended by Thornton & Doty. A motion for a new trial was filed and taken under advisement by Judge Britton. On June 18 Coffee made his third statement to the two ministers, Rev. G.T. Phillips of Graysville, and Rev. J.T. Jackson, of Crawfordsville. In this he said that James R. Rankin did the killing with *a revolver, and Monday Rankin, his son, John Curtis, James Dennis and himself were along. The house was searched, several articles carried away, and $300 in money secured. When the crowd separated, "old man Rankin" held his pistol at Coffee's head, and said, "If you ever tell I will kill you." This statement was sworn to by Rev. Jackson in the court on July 1, and was placed on file as a supplementary motion for a new trial, which was also overruled. On May 19 Judge Britton had Coffee and Dennis brought to the court-house, and, after announcing that the motion for a new trial was overruled in both cases, he sentenced them to be hanged on Thursday, Sept. 3, Dennis attorneys appealed to the Supreme Court. As the court did not convene until after the day set for the hanging, Governor Gray reprieved them both until Oct. 16. The Supreme Court granted a new trial to Dennis on the grounds that the third statement might cause a jury to return a different verdict than they had. In the last few days Coffee has stated that Mrs. Rankin and her daughter, Mollie, knew all about the murder, and knew that it was to be committed.*

If that part of the story wasn't strange enough, there is lots more. When John was taken to be hanged, he continued to try to convince the authorities of his innocence. When they had secured the rope to his neck and dropped the body, by some trick of the rope or interference, the rope broke, and his body fell to the ground. The guards not to be stopped from doing the job set before them, he was brought up and once again secured to the rope. This time, when the body dropped and by some miracle the rope broke again, they caught the body before it hit the ground.

On the third attempt, a volunteer from the crowd came up to release his body should the rope not hold this time. The rope did hold that time, however, and Mr. Coffee finally met his end. The man who pushed Coffee for his final drop received a payment of $1,000, and some referred to this as blood money and cursed, as it wasn't long after this that the man became overcome with an incurable disease and died.

New York Times, *October 17, 1885*
No such scene as was witnessed on the scaffold at Crawfordsville at noon today, probably ever was witnessed in this vicinity. Last January James McMullen and his wife were murdered in a most diabolical manner. John W. Coffee was arrested for the crime. During his incarceration he made three different confessions, one of which sought to throw the blame for the killing on James M. Dennis, a respected farmer. Dennis was

SCENE OF THE McMULLEN TRAGEDY.

A drawing of the scene of the McMullen tragedy in the newspaper. *Courtesy of the Crawfordsville District Public Library.*

arrested and convicted upon Coffee's testimony, together with a web of circumstantial evidence, skillfully woven around him. The two men were condemned to be hanged on the 3rd day of September. Dennis protested his innocence from the first. Before the day set for the execution Coffee made a third confession in which he implicated James Rankin, Monday Rankin, James M. Dennis and John Curtis. He declared that James Rankin did the killing with a navy revolver firing four shots. It was on the strength of this third confession that the Governor respited Coffee and Dennis until today. The Supreme Court afterward granted Dennis a new trial. James Rankin proved an unquestionable alibi. Dennis will probably be released from custody without another trial. Coffee was hanged today. The streets were crowded with people from all parts of the county. The Sheriff had issued 200 invitations and about that number of spectators were admitted into the enclosure surrounding the gallows at 9 o'clock this morning. Coffee was utterly prostrated and refused to be consoled by his spiritual adviser. He had refused to eat any food since last night. His condition at that time was most pitiable. Dennis was removed to an adjoining county as a precaution against a possible mob. At 11 o'clock Coffee having braced up somewhat in the meanwhile, made some additions to his third confession implicating others in the crime but his statements are not believed. When the time came for the execution he had a spasm and he had to be half carried to the scaffold. When the rope was placed around his neck he talked incoherently repeating his implication of others. When the drop fell the rope broke and the body dropped to the ground. The neck was not broken but blood oozed from the condemned man's ears. He was carried up on the scaffold and while the rope was being readjusted he recovered consciousness and begged to have the cap taken off that he might make another speech. This request was refused. When the drop again fell the rope broke a second time, but the body was caught before it fell to the ground. It was lifted up and held in the arms of Deputy Sheriffs while the rope was fixed for the third time. When the drop fell again the rope held and Coffee strangled to death in 12 minutes. The spectacle was sickening. The Governor said today that after investigating the case he had become satisfied that Coffee alone was guilty of the murder.

After his death, John wasn't satisfied remaining in his grave and made several visits to the area. He was sighted by several who knew him walking around the towns of the county and even hitched a ride with both a farmer and the train. Even to this day, some say he is still seen around the jail and grounds where he met his fate.

Newport Hoosier State, *October 28, 1885*
Superstition
The ghost of John W. Coffee, who was hanged at Crawfordsville on the 16th of this month, has already been seen by a number of persons prowling around in the vicinity of Elmdale, where the tragedy was committed. The ghost stopped an old farmer after night and rode about three miles with him, and just as he was opposite the ruins of the McMullen house, hopped out and bounded away with the speed of a jack-rabbit. Some of the timid ones in the neighborhood are now afraid to venture out after night.

Jefferson Daily Evening News, *November 11, 1885*
An Indiana Ghost
The Lafayette Courier *says that Dick Tracy, the L.N.A. & C. conductor, who claims that he saw the ghost of Coffee with a rope around his neck and covered with blood, on his caboose, has not made a trip since. He is thoroughly frightened, and told a friend all about it at his home, corner of Halsted and Forty-third Streets, Chicago. He and his brakeman, Wm. Buss, were in the caboose, when the ghost jumped on the front end just as they were leaving Crawfordsville. Tracy rushed and locked the door of the car, when the ghost climbed on the roof and came in the cupola and took a seat in the car. The rope was around his neck, his*

THE EXECUTION OF JOHN W. C. COFFEE.

A drawing of the scene of the execution of John W.C. Coffee. *Courtesy of the Crawfordsville District Public Library.*

face was bloody and his hands were tied behind him. He rode for about thirty miles, while they sat transfixed with fear. He then went through the back door, jumped off, and they saw him run up the steep embankment and disappear.

Was John Coffee a murderer or an innocent man? That may never be known, but if you happen to meet him some night wandering the area, perhaps you could ask him.

PART III

HAUNTINGS

ROTARY JAIL

In 1881, the very first rotary jail in the United States of America was built in Crawfordsville, and it remains one of only three still able to operate. It began to accept prisoners in 1882 and continued to hold prisoners until 1973, when it was closed. It could hold a maximum of thirty-seven inmates while requiring only two deputies to monitor them. It was an interesting design created by William H. Brown and Benjamin F. Haugh of Indianapolis. Its design allowed the cells to be completely sealed off for the most part and only one inmate released at a time. This made it almost impossible to escape and kept the guards working the jail much safer. It was specifically placed to be close to the courthouse for quick and cheap transport of prisoners back and forth. The concept was to be extremely secure without requiring much manpower to save the community money. The design even allowed inmates to have indoor plumbing before many of the homes in town got it. It was the very first building in Crawfordsville constructed to receive electricity so that it could be immediately put on the grid when the city was ready to use it. As such, the light fixtures in the sheriff's residence were made to hold either gas or electricity.

Years later, in 1939, the *Indianapolis Star* reported that because of the design, the jail was listed as one of fifteen county jails in Indiana that were unfit for human habitation. The downside to the design related to heating and cooling. It became extremely cold or hot, depending on the time of the year. Many of the inmates were picked up for being drunk, and so they were hot-blooded. This issue caused many of those who were locked

The rotary jail. *Photo by authors.*

inside to lay as close to the bars as possible to get fresh cool air from the windows located on the outer walls. This, combined with the machinery rotating the cells being virtually quiet, caused many severe injuries to the sleeping inmates. There were several attempts to repair or even replace the jail, but in June 1973, the inmates were transferred to a new county jail. Shortly after it was no longer being used as a jail, the Tannenbaum family purchased the property to stop it from being destroyed. In May 1975, the old jail was placed in the National Register of Historic Places and was included in the Historic American Engineering Record. It was also in 1975 that the Montgomery County Cultural Foundation was started to preserve the jail and turn it into a museum.

The jail housed two hangings during its time, the first being John Coffee on October 15, 1885, and the second being John C. Henning on May 27, 1886. After Henning's death, the inmates of the jail claimed they could hear him crying and wailing in the cells. They pleaded to be let go so they wouldn't have to hear his laments any longer.

One of the cells of the rotary jail. *Photo by authors.*

Many people believe that John Coffee can still be seen on certain nights on the grounds of the jail. They say that they feel his presence when they visit the jail for a tour or some other event. He has been sighted in many places since his death, but he always seems to come back to the jail to check on those who may visit the place. Many residents of the jail, both inmates and others, recall waking up to gospel music playing near dawn. Even to this day, if you listen quietly near sunrise, you might hear gospel music being played or sung. John was a devout man, and it is thought that he continues to sing his songs even now that he has passed on. Is he praising the Lord beyond the grave or just filling the air with beautiful music to say hello to the new sun rising?

Sometimes visitors and the like see a little girl roaming the jail. She is mainly seen in the basement or on the second floor. She is known to be nice and either singing or laughing. What would keep a child around after their passing on in such a place? If you happen to see her smiling face, don't be scared; it may just brighten your day.

Some say one of the sheriffs is still on duty some nights, and if you are on the top floor, you may see him still in uniform as he walks around the building. Many hear things such as voices or other strange sounds besides seeing dark figures and such. To some, the experiences they have are nice and gentle, while to others, they are dark and unfriendly.

What causes such a different reaction for each person we might never know, but the jail seems to have a weight or loudness about it that you can feel if you are there long enough, according to just about anyone who walks into the place. If you are ever in the area around Halloween and a nighttime tour is up your alley, you may be surprised by what you see, hear or feel.

MAIN STREET'S GHOST

In Crawfordsville, the downtown area has had lots of stories and history over the years of paranormal activity. We have a lot of buildings from as far back as the 1800s, not to mention the early 1900s. The city has seen its share of changes and renovations, especially since at one point a major fire destroyed a great portion of it, but many of the buildings are nearly the same as when they were first built.

Downtown Crawfordsville has tons of history and interesting things that have happened, as it is the true heart of the city. One interesting event that happened was back in 2012, when a video popped up online about a ghost on Main Street. Main Street, as well as lots of other places downtown, is well known for its paranormal sightings and events. We have had a little bit of everything from spirits walking down the street, mediums giving séances and strange cryptid sightings. This video is different mostly in the respect of it being actual evidence to confuse and scare the local populace. This video was of someone using a camera or phone to record a stationary video screen, most likely a security camera feed. The video shows downtown Crawfordsville, at night, on Main Street looking from the north to the south side of the street. You see a local bank in the video and a few other buildings. It is interesting that you don't see a single person or vehicle in the time of the video, even if it is brief, as Main Street is one of the many important ways through the heart of this town. The video shows something flying through the air before making several changes to its location. It darts almost down to the road at one point. It seems to come from nowhere and suddenly

Main Street and the location of the ghost sighting. *Photo by authors.*

appears in the sky. This video kept people asking lots of questions for a brief time in the town before, like most things, the story faded from memory. The interesting thing about this story goes a little further. Several people who saw more of the original video feed before it was recorded and put online speak of something else being seen. They claim to see what looks like a young girl in an old-style dress leaning on the windows of the building in the video before darting off into the darkness of the building.

It brings us back to the question: is the video proof of a haunting or something else entirely? You can search on YouTube for Crawfordsville, Indiana Main Street Ghost and decide for yourself.

JEFFERSON STREET

There is a history of hauntings happening in homes, businesses, graveyards and so on, but we have much fewer stories about haunted streets. The concept isn't foreign to us but is a much lesser-known phenomenon. The phenomenon has been glorified in movies and television about a small area or city block having some type of energy or spirit that haunts and torments people. It is well documented that we have stories about haunted roads or even highways throughout the world, but a city street in the middle of town much less so. We find stories of things being seen moving along the roadside, such as women in white or creatures in the darkness, but what about stories of ghosts that seem to take joy in visiting each house on a street they choose to haunt?

Jefferson Street in Crawfordsville seems to have just such a ghost haunting it. This street, in the middle of town, has many old homes on it, as it is an older section of the city. Some of these homes can be found to date back to the turn of the twentieth century. Many have seen multiple remodelings over the years. It is not far from the middle school in town and has had many stories throughout the years. It is interesting that this street is mentioned in each report as being the location for the sighting or sightings.

Each story is eerily similar and about a young boy. This boy is obviously a spirit or ghost, as he is seen wearing either old Victorian clothing or an old-type school uniform. He is pasty white and luminous. The boy stays around usually for a minute or two when seen and has been seen by entire groups of people. Even though there have been numerous sightings on the

Jefferson Street. *Photo by authors.*

street, most of them originate from the different homes in the area. The time of year seems to play little to no part in the sightings, and very few people become scared or have any ill feelings in seeing him. Why he is here no one knows, but maybe one day someone will get a word with him and let the rest of us know.

DOWNTOWN FURNITURE STORE

Like in many small towns, Crawfordsville can be stuck in the past when referring to businesses that have changed names many times. There are some who refer to a certain gas station as Super Test. The same can be said of the downtown furniture store, forever known to many as the Old Schloots Furniture store, even though the name has changed three times. This old building was once the home of Graham Busy Store. It was owned by George W. Graham, and he had some of the cheapest prices in town, or so his ads were known to say. He had a war with another local store in regard to who had the cheapest stock. The stores and people involved kept up this fight even after Graham's death in 1908. The building has been in use as one thing or another since it was built in 1881.

Sometimes when a building is this old, it seems to grab the energy of those who come through it, work in it or just visit. One former employee recalls hearing women's voices chattering away on the third floor. When she told Mr. Schloot, he said the building had been a theater before he bought it and that the room where she heard the voices was the alterations department.

A former employee recalls a time when they were working and an elderly lady came in wearing a pillbox hat and an old brown coat. As the employee walked to the spot to attempt to help her, the lady vanished, and no manner of searching the building could locate her.

The doors and rocking chairs are prone to moving on their own, and people say they knew that a visitor was there but they just couldn't see them.

The downtown furniture store. *Photo by authors.*

So it became the practice to say "hi" and "goodbye" to them as the door opened or the chairs moved.

The old princess phone on the second floor had a dial tone years after it had been turned off, and no one could explain why. The lights were known to have issues with turning on and off on their own, and any floor that a person stepped on before the lights were turned on seemed to have a presence waiting in the dark.

Were these just weird happenings that could easily be explained away, or was this old building still holding a small portion of its visitors over the hundred-plus years of its life?

MYSTERIOUS LIGHTS

In 1890, there were reports of a mysterious light that seemed to haunt the farms around Crawfordsville. This light was seen for over six years almost every night illuminating places that would have had no light of their own. People saw the light move of its own accord as well as sit for fixed amounts of time. What could possibly be lighting up houses and buildings in a time of low electricity? At the time, people were more aware of their surroundings and knew when something was off.

Crawfordsville Daily Journal, *January 28, 1890*
Two Mysterious Lights
One haunts a dead man's house for six Years while Another Makes a Man Believe His House is on fire.
A farmer from the neighborhood about 3½ miles north of here was in town Saturday and told some remarkable things about a mysterious light which haunts that region. About six years ago Burton Dazy died and ever since then until within the last few months this illumination has haunted the house of the dead man and the whole neighborhood about. On one occasion a party of persons were passing the house about 11 o'clock at night and they observed a light in it. They knew no one was inside unless it be an intruder for the occupants were of the party. Two of the persons slowly approached the haunted dwelling keeping their eyes closely fixed all the time on the light. They got close up to the window looked in and the room appeared as if illuminated by electricity but the source of the illumination

could not be discovered. Finally the rest of the party came up and it was decided to search the house but the light suddenly disappeared and all was darkness. The search went on however, but nothing was found to explain the wonderful apparition. After that the light would be seen, around the wood house, the smoke house and other places in the vicinity. Sometimes a lone rider would see it arise in the midst of a grove nearby, stand still a few moments, then silently, slowly but surely move off and disappear. One night it shown [sic] through the window at the home of Charles Dazy after the family had retired and made every object in the room visible. Mr. Dazy opened the door to discover the source and suddenly all was black night again. The house is now occupied by Frank Shepherd. S.H. Gregg hearing the above story recalled another mysterious light which some years ago made its appearance on the farm of John Munns, four miles west. One night Arch Martin and his wife were coming home and when they were a mile away saw the house, for all appearances, to be in flames and burning down. Mr. Martin whipped up his horses until they went at a 2:40 gait keeping his eyes all the time on the house. It still appeared to be burning but just before reaching home he had to drive down into a gully out of sight of the house. When the house came in sight again the flames had disappeared and a careful search failed to show any evidence of any fire. The same light giving the impression of a conflagration was often seen after that and many a time, persons in that neighborhood thought a house, barn, or forest was on fire. It is very likely that both these strange apparitions can be explained by the fact that they appear in the region of marshes. The marsh gas or "will o' the wisp" act very much like those above described.

THE MONON HOTEL

The Monon Hotel opened on North Green Street in the heart of downtown Crawfordsville in August 1927. At that time, it had all the top amenities, including baths, telephone services and hot and cold running water. It was highly decorated and furnished and was considered a jewel of the town. Opening day drew a crowd of over two hundred citizens to the building. As with many hotels, over the years it has changed hands many times. Currently, the Monon is home to Backstep Brewing Company, a local brewery owned and operated by two former firemen.

The Monon Hotel. *Photo by authors.*

Inside the Monon Hotel (now the Backstep Brewing Company). *Photo by authors.*

The upstairs (hotel) portion of the building was condemned in the late '70s, but some residents have refused to leave. Some say that as you enter the upper portions of the building, you begin to feel more uncomfortable and uneasy. People have reported being pinched by unseen hands and explicitly yelled at for being too loud by bodiless voices. Down in the bar, workers have heard the food service bells ringing by themselves, a Wheel of Fortune game spinning on its own and the sounds of footsteps coming from the empty floors above. In the basement, which contains a covered entrance to the tunnels under Crawfordsville, employees have heard sighs from behind them when they are working down there alone.

Thousands have traveled through these doors (including, some say, notorious gangster John Dillinger), and lives have been changed and lost within its walls. With all of this history, it is no wonder that some claim the past hasn't quite let go of the Monon Hotel.

NORTH DONNELLEY'S

In 1921, Richard R. Donnelley opened a factory in Crawfordsville to print books. Donnelley's, as the business was called, had been in business for fifty-seven years at that point and was destined for greatness. It expanded over time until not one, but two factories existed in the town. The original building became known as North Donnelley's and had a large tower that people could see from all over town. Many of the people of Crawfordsville have worked at Donnelley's over the years before and after its name changes.

The people who work there say that the history has lain thick on the building, and it seems some of its old workers continue to come to work even after they have passed on from this life. The presses that make Bibles

North Donnelley's tower. *Photo by authors.*

have been known to be visited by one of the old-timers who worked at the press for many years. In the old clinic, you can still smell the sick people who visited the place. The storage for large rolls of paper has been known to give people the creeps with the energy in the area.

The tower is probably one of the most interesting spots to visit for a few reasons. One of those is a little girl who is regularly seen in and near the place, playing. The old entrance into the tower was strictly off-limits to all but security but somehow remains perfectly clean. It holds the old trophies and first-edition books of the company. What spirit is visiting to continue cleaning the building that it loved? This factory may not be the oldest building in the city, but it remains one of the ones with the strangest energies connected to it. Do we have a case of overimagination in an old building, or do those who have come before still come to work to help out?

THE TRESTLES

On a street in Crawfordsville, between two factories and just down the road from the college, rests a train trestle. Like lots of these places, people tell stories about it and feel creeped out by being in the location for long. This particular trestle has an interesting story attached to it. It looks dark even in daylight because of its design and the location of trees around it—and maybe it hides from the sun.

The trestle. *Photo by authors.*

Some who visit it say that if you are there at the right time of night, a person appears to be hanging from underneath the trestle. Who is this mysterious spirit that nightly must suffer through its last gruesome moments? This trestle is very large, but those who drive under it swear that the feet of the spirit can be heard sliding across the tops of their cars as they make their way under it.

Another trestle that has a lot of strangeness to it is known as the New Market trestle. Visitors have been known to hear the sounds of train whistles as well as see strange blue lights around it on any given night. It was the home of a horrible train accident, or so the locals will tell you when they talk about it. Is it truly haunted by the train that crashed there, or is it just another legend of this strange area?

THE VANITY THEATER

The Vanity Theater is home to the Sugar Creek Players Acting Troupe in Crawfordsville. This building was deeded to the Sugar Creek Players in 1983 after having been a motion picture theater also called the Vanity. The Sugar Creek Players opened their new home with the show *Crimes of the Heart*. After a lot of work and remodeling, the building became a great place to take in a show.

The building didn't start as a theater of any kind but instead started as a farm implement business in the 1890s before later housing both a department

The Vanity Theater. *Photo by authors.*

store and a car dealership. It became a movie theater in the 1930s and stayed that way until the early 1950s. It mostly sat empty until the '80s. As with any building that is old in the area, it is full of stories and legends.

Those who visit the building tell many stories about things that happen there. Before the remodel of the upstairs, in what used to be the old costume room, things seemed to fly off the racks or topple over on their own. People have even had things such as hats thrown at them. The building floors are old and make a lot of noise anytime someone walks down the hallway. It is common to hear people running around upstairs when everyone is downstairs and no one should be upstairs to be making the noises. Some have told stories of bad things happening as well, such as being pushed down the stairs and feeling threatened by a strange energy.

There is a story told by the people who have worked there about George, the theater ghost. He was believed to have hanged himself from the catwalk. When you walk around the theater, you always feel eyes watching you. You're never alone there, some say.

OTHER HAUNTINGS

If you have time to take in a few of the old newspapers from the late 1800s and early 1900s, you will come across numerous accounts of local citizens reporting that their houses were haunted. It seems that mostly it was the ghost of a former husband or wife who, for some reason, came back to torment their mourning spouses. The dead in Crawfordsville were not content to move on to their final resting places and would much rather hang about, throwing rocks, knocking over furniture or scaring loved ones.

One of the most widely known haunted places in Crawfordsville was the old Baptist church. It was a small cabin that stood on the land where the electric company now resides. Everyone around town knew this place to be the home of spirits and kept a wide berth around it at night. That is, until a local minister decided to visit and rid the place of its otherworldly residents. While there, he discovered the remains of a local vagabond partially buried in the floor, and further investigations from the police revealed that two local doctors had been using the place to store stolen remains from the cemetery and practice various medical skills with them because the cost of legally obtained cadavers was too expensive. They had concocted the story of the haunted church and spread the rumors, all while flashing candlelight in the windows at night and making noises when people got close to ensure that their tale was believed.

In 1900, the local newspapers reported a story that the janitor of the Mace Methodist Church got the surprise of his life one night while sweeping up in the furnace room. Homer Linn claimed that an old suit that had once belonged to a Mr. Coulter was dancing around in demonic glee and uttering vile words about fellow parishioners. Mace has several other stories about spirits visiting its locals, including Mr. John Sellars, who saw ghosts and spirits on several occasions about town but vowed not to run away from them anymore. There are many more stories like this in the papers of this time; it was not unheard of for sightings to be documented in this way.

PART IV

PLACES OF THE DEAD AND DYING

PLACES OF THE DEAD AND DYING

There are lots of stories across the country of locations that housed people during their last days. These locations usually have some strange and interesting things reported from the staff and visitors. Is it those who passed on but didn't want to leave? Is this energy that is left over when people die, but with so many deaths it starts to gather and create weak spots in the veil? We have several such places in Crawfordsville, including hospitals, nursing homes, assisted living facilities and even cemeteries. These are spots that attract the mysterious and cause us to take care to show reverence and respect to those who are closer to the other side or have recently passed on.

THE OLD CULVER HOSPITAL

On the northeast side of Crawfordsville, there rests a building complex with a mysterious history. It has as many, if not more, stories than the rest of the city all together. This building is well known to the locals, and most can give you a story about it, as it plays an important role in the history of the town. Culver Union Hospital, or the old Culver Hospital to the locals, was built in 1902 and named for L.L. Culver, who donated greatly to its construction.

The building has been repeatedly expanded and remodeled. Up until 1984, it was a hospital, and then it became an apartment building. While it was the hospital, it had its own morgue and also a psychiatric clinic. It was finally closed entirely after being determined to be unsafe. In recent years, it has once again been remodeled and opened as apartments. A great many people who have visited during the years or lived there at one time after it was remodeled have told stories of the building and the spirits they believe still walk the grounds.

Many claim to have seen a woman in white in the upper floors of the building walking around, looking out the windows and even being seen on the roof at times. People routinely report that things in their apartments move on their own or even seem to break or fall apart right before their eyes. There have also been reports that it is not beyond normal to catch a glimpse of what must have been a former patient walking around a corner or through a doorway. Residents have reported hearing children where there are none.

An older picture of Culver Hospital before its original expansion. *Courtesy of the Crawfordsville District Public Library.*

Those who have been brave enough to enter the basement, where the morgue once was, claim it gives you a creepy feeling down there, like you're being watched. They tend to feel hard pressed to go any farther and immediately go back upstairs. The morgue was still intact even after its first transition into an apartment complex but has recently been removed with the last remodel.

Down in the basement, it's said that there are what appear to be sealed-up holes that some suspect may have once led to an extensive tunnel system. These tunnels are believed to exist throughout the old downtown of Crawfordsville, and little is known about what they would have been used for. Few who venture to the place come back without a story to tell about hearing or seeing something odd.

We have a story that comes from a former resident of the apartment complex now called the Historic Whitlock Place. She says that one night shortly after moving in, she was taking a relaxing bath while on the phone discussing the stories and rumors about the place. She had a floral arrangement that was extremely well put together in her bathroom for decoration. As the conversation went on, all of a sudden this floral arrangement split exactly in half, with half falling next to the tub. As it was impossible to divide exactly in the middle, and for such a strongly built arrangement to break at all, the lady was left in a state of confusion, and she quickly ended her phone call and got out of the bathroom. The experience really freaked out the lady, and she was even more disturbed knowing this was her only bathroom to use in her apartment.

Many claim that the old hospital is the most haunted place in the area. It has attracted many people to sometimes illegally enter the premises over the years to do their own paranormal investigations. One resident of the town tells us about a time he and his friends attempted to do just that. He says that he and his friends took some recording equipment into the facility at night and split up to investigate all the areas. They all claim to have heard the sounds of gurneys moving throughout the halls the entire night, loudly screeching their wheels. However, after leaving the building, they found that all their recordings were damaged and unusable. Not to be deterred, that young man went back the next night by himself to investigate further. He went down into the boiler room and wasn't there very long before he heard an inhuman voice ask, "Why are you here?" He immediately tried to leave but noticed doors opening and shutting on his

A picture of Culver Hospital before its last remodel. *Photo by authors.*

way out and figured that his friends were there after all and were playing tricks on him. He went to one of the doors and tried to open it, but it felt like a game of tug-of-war, with someone on the other side holding it shut. He announced loudly that he was leaving, and the door slowly started to open. He could see a pair of yellow eyes peering out at him. Thoroughly frightened by now, he took off for the door he'd come in through only to find it had been barricaded from the outside. Once he finally made it out of the building, he vowed he'd never go back.

Another story about a family who decided to do their own investigation of the hospital also ended in a vow to never return. The family says that they felt watched and stalked the entire time they were in the building and even after leaving felt like something had followed them home. They went so far as to have a cleansing done on their home in order to rid themselves of what they felt was an evil presence that came from the old hospital.

BEN HUR NURSING HOME

There is a nursing home in Crawfordsville that has had lots of reported stories throughout the life of the town. Ben Hur Nursing Home was an old dairy farm before being purchased and used by the Ben Hur Life Association. The association owned and operated out of it until they sold it. While they did, they used the buildings for living units for their elderly members until it was purchased by Martha Williams. Williams was the mother of Esther Houston, who later ran and owned the nursing home. It was then passed down to her two sons, David and Daniel Houston. The nursing home has housed many residents in its time, including some who claim to have noticed some strange things happening.

Some of the residents say they see a nurse walking the halls that isn't completely there. They believe she is a nurse who worked there years before

Ben Hur Nursing Home before it became the nursing home. *Courtesy of the Crawfordsville District Public Library.*

and is continuing her work after her own passing. The residents also tell lots of stories about those who are about to pass constantly being bothered by both a young girl and a young boy that no one else can see. The staff claims that when this begins to happen, it isn't long until that resident will pass on. Are these children a warning of something, or is it just the imaginations of those close to death?

There is also a story from a resident who lived there who had firsthand knowledge of the children running around the building. They said that the children seem to visit a person days before a death would happen in the place and there would be no end in their bugging of this person until finally the resident would pass on. However, even when they passed on, many reported that the children could still be seen in that room for days afterward.

THE OLD OAK HILL CEMETERY

The old Oak Hill Cemetery, as many in the area still call it, was built in 1875 after many of the graves were moved there from other cemeteries in the town of Crawfordsville. It is the final resting place of several of the town's most well-known residents. General Lewis "Lew" Wallace and his wife are buried there and were some of the best-known Crawfordsville citizens. He was the eleventh governor of New Mexico Territory, and he served as a major general for the Union army in the Civil War. He was also the famous author who wrote *Ben-Hur: A Tale of the Christ*. It was one of the most famous books written in the 1800s and has several movies made about it. His wife was just as famous as an author, having written six books and many articles in magazines and other publications.

There is a story in the legends of Crawfordsville that tells of a woman whose young child died while lost in the woods. The child got lost while out on a family outing. Knowing that when you get lost, you shouldn't wander farther around, the child sat down beside a tree to wait to be found and sadly froze to death before being discovered the following day. After the burial of the child, the family had a monument erected with a chair on it. This was to allow the mother to be with her child every day. The woman is said to have visited her child nightly, singing songs and telling stories to the child. One morning, the mother was found to have dug up the body and taken her own life while holding and rocking her child. The legend says that if you visit the grave and sit on the chair and find it warm, then the mother has recently visited. The legend goes on to say that if the chair is warm when

Old Oak Hill Cemetery. *Photo by authors.*

The chair in old Oak Hill Cemetery. *Photo by authors.*

you are sitting on it, you will die in seven years. This story or legend has many similarities with lots of others throughout Indiana and other places. Which is the true story, or is there a true story? We may never know, but it is interesting that so many similar stories appear throughout the ages and across the nation.

Oak Hill Cemetery also plays home to the spirit of one Madame Irma Van Rokey, who, according to legend and sightings from around the turn of the century, makes the cemetery and surrounding area her home. Many say she has been seen to walk the cemetery and even down to the Sperry Bridge. Her life was tragically taken from her in the Monon train wreck of 1892. She died far from her home of Austria. She was a member of the City Club Vaudeville and Burlesque Company and was on her way to play a show in Chicago when the train wreck happened. She tragically lost her life and was buried in an unmarked grave in Oak Hill Cemetery. From there, many farmhands from nearby recall seeing her. Does she still visit the graveyard to this day, or has she finally moved on to the next adventure?

POTTS CEMETERY

Potts Cemetery just outside Crawfordsville isn't well known. It was established in 1810 and is just a few minutes outside the town toward Waynetown. This cemetery houses some very interesting gravestones, including one that is made out of metal and looks like it's been shot at some point, as a bullet hole clearly stands out on the surface. What's even more interesting, however, is that the area of Old 55 that the cemetery sits near has had a lot of strange sightings over the years, from spirits to giant flying creatures in the sky.

Legend has it that the cemetery is haunted by the spirit of a young girl. This girl can sometimes be seen by those driving by or visiting the cemetery. One firsthand account tells of a man driving down the road one evening on his way home from work. As he rounded the graveyard, he saw something that shook him for a moment, but after closer examination, he felt it could only be a young girl playing among the gravestones. The girl was wearing older clothes and seemed to be out of place, as well as time, as she moved around. He quickly went on his way but brought up the story again later with some people he knew, only to hear that several people had seen her at one time or another. This cemetery seems to be the playground for one of its residents even after she has passed on. Why she is sighted here, we might not ever know, but if you are driving down Old 55 by Potts Cemetery some night, take a look and see if you can catch sight of her playing around the tombstones.

Potts Cemetery. *Photo by authors.*

The road that Potts Cemetery is on, just off Old 55, is not a very long one. However, for such a short distance, it has a long history of strange sightings. One family, while out driving at night, spotted what they described as a giant white bat flying around the area. They claimed it was roughly nine feet long and had a sixteen-foot wingspan. Another passerby claims to have seen a giant black gargoyle-like creature in the area. What could these creatures be? Why are they attracted to this short stretch of road? Are you brave enough to take a drive and find out?

CRAWFORDSVILLE'S MASONIC CEMETERY

The Masonic Cemetery was founded in 1866 but was acquired by Oak Hill Cemetery in 1997. It is interesting that even though this cemetery is older, the folks of Crawfordsville prefer to call the other Oak Hill the "old Oak Hill Cemetery." This cemetery sits on the main road through the city and is a beautiful site to visit when you travel through town, even though it is a cemetery. Many residents of the area will tell you the history of their families and which of the three Oak Hill Cemeteries their families are buried in. This cemetery, you would think, would be without many stories, being that its location is in the middle of the city and it is probably one of

Crawfordsville Masonic Cemetery. *Photo by authors.*

the least spooky-looking cemeteries, but no part of Crawfordsville seems to be without some type of story of the strange and possibly paranormal.

Many nights, people claim to see not just shadows moving among the stones but also orbs floating through the air. What makes these orbs interesting is that a camera is seldom needed to see them floating through the air. What are these orbs? Are they spirits, energy or something we have no name for? We don't know, but many people of the area will tell you a story about the orbs they have seen as they snuck into the graveyard late at night or just happened to be passing on foot or vehicle.

PART V

THE HAUNTED VALLEY

THE VALLEY

There is a place just outside the town of Crawfordsville that is used to scare the locals their entire childhoods. In the past, there were haunted hayrides that traveled through this area, giving additional life to the eeriness of this place. This is what is known as the "haunted valley." There is no part of it that people don't talk about in their legends and stories, and it is widely known that spirits and more walk there at night. It has had a little bit of everything over the years. The valley rests down a steep hill and ends at a decently large creek. Sugar Creek is just on one side and Rattlesnake Creek on the other. A lone bridge crosses the creek leading you up the road. Farther on up the road rests a cemetery that is closed for visitors for some mysterious reason. It always has the entrance fenced off, with "private property" signs, as well as signs that claim it is government property and trespassers will be shot. What about this graveyard could possibly be a reason to keep people out of it? Extremely strange creatures have been seen in the area from Bigfoot-like creatures to large flying creatures that might be the legendary thunderbird. It's been claimed that in the past, witches were burned in the valley. It was also noted in the old newspapers that a Native American witch doctor lived on the land and treated those who had been possessed of demonic spirits by boiling urine and oil to tease the spirits out of their bodies.

Spooky Hollow

There is a bridge in Montgomery County that every child born before the 2000s knows. It is the center of all hidden and haunted stories about things that go bump in the night in this neck of the woods. The bridge rests in the valley and has been through many changes over the years. It was a wooden bridge before being changed into a metal one. It finally became all concrete and steel in recent years, and some of the mysteriousness about the bridge seems to have lifted, or maybe the concrete bridge just isn't as scary to the mind as an old metal or wooden bridge can be late at night. The stories change over the years about the old bridge, but a similarity stays.

One story believed to have come from the mid-1800s is of a man who had left the woman he loved to fight in the Civil War. When he returned, he found out that she had married someone else while he was away. Distraught thinking about going on without her, he tied a rope around a beam on the bridge with one end around his neck and jumped to his death. Many say that when the wind blows just right, you can hear his body thumping against the bridge.

Another story tells how sometime in the past, an African American man was hanged from the rafters of one of the older bridges that sat on this spot. It was rumored that years after the incident, travelers to the bridge at night could see an old rope hanging from the metal bridge, a reminder of the gruesome deed.

The final stories are similar to other stories told around the country and make you start to wonder if it is a retelling from somewhere else, a true story that keeps happening or just an urban legend used to frighten us. A couple

Spooky Hollow Bridge. *Photo by authors.*

were out for a drive when they crossed the bridge. The boy, trying to play a trick, stopped the car and told his girlfriend that the car had broken down. It wasn't long after that they heard a strange noise above the car. He confessed his prank to his girlfriend but assured her that the noise was not part of it. Feeling that he should investigate to make up for the prank, he got out of the car. He wasn't gone long when the noise returned. The girl jumped out of the car to see what was happening and saw him bloodied, hanging from a beam above the car, swinging back and forth in the wind. His feet were scraping on the top of the car. People now say that because of this, if you stop your car with your lights shining on the bridge late at night and flash your lights three times, you will see the ghostly body swinging above the bridge. Other people say that cars are known to unexplainably die with their lights flashing. This bridge is also known to be Montgomery County's home to a version of the story of a woman in white, or la Llorona. A long time ago, a distraught mother drowned her children in the creek, and now if you stop your car on the bridge, flash your lights and honk your horn three times, she will appear. They say you should never shut your car off, or else she will come and drown you too. If you do shut your car off, you should put it in neutral, and the spirits of those she has claimed will push your car to safety.

OFFIELD MONUMENT

In 1821, William Offield built a cabin on a creek. This creek later became known as Offield Creek, and the area is just outside what is now Crawfordsville. William Offield was the first person to set up residence in what became known as Montgomery County. He came from Tennessee with his wife and one child. The location of his cabin was perfect, as the creek not far away poured into Sugar Creek and his land was surrounded on two sides by water. William went on to be one of the three first county commissioners, alongside James Blevins and John McCollough. Being that this was the first

The Offield Monument. *Photo by authors.*

location of settlement in the county, it is only natural that a monument was erected. It was first erected in the field where the house sat before being moved to the edge of the field so people could more easily see it as they passed along the road. The monument was erected in 1881 by Sidney Speed to honor and recognize William Offield, who had died earlier that year.

Several stories are told of the monument. One of them is that if you read the monument by candlelight at midnight on Halloween, the dates will change. Another story is that if you feel the stone and it is warm to the touch, you are doomed to die soon. The stone is creepy to some and a cool monument to others, but to all, it is a piece of history to be seen and remembered.

HIBERNIAN MILL

On Sugar Creek in the haunted valley area, across from where Offield Monument sits, was the site of the Hibernian Mill. This mill was known as the haunted mill back in the late 1800s to early 1900s. Everyone around knew that it was haunted and often came to see what would happen. Several stories were even talked about in the local papers.

Crawfordsville Daily Journal, *July 7, 1892*
Gay Picnic Party
Early this morning a gay party of young ladies left for a day in the woods near the haunted Hibernian mill where the spook delights to show himself the year around. The party was composed of the following young ladies: Misses Joan Elston, Gertrude Beck, Mand Mahorney, May Taylor, Jessie Lee, Ethel Barhill, Edith Bryant, Agnes Chamberlain, Bess Nicholson, Hattie Hauser and Ada Somerville. The party was chaperoned by Misses Sellie Newton and Mande Cowan.

Even the Famous Crawfordsville Ghost Club told a story in one of its meetings about the spirit that haunted the mill.

THE AEROLITE

T he valley has some interesting articles written about it, but one especially stands out as either a joke or a strange bit of news. An aerolite, something like a meteor, was believed to be seen falling, but when the hole was searched where it landed, a couple of blue bunnies and pink snakes were described to be found. Was this some kind of joke written up, or was it the work of fairies messing with our heads?

Crawfordsville Weekly Journal, *April 1, 1893*
An Aerolite
It Sizzled Through the Air Last Night Blinding and Terrorizing Two Men on a Lonely Road
Mr. Carmichael, of Chicago, is an agent for the Deering binder. He arrived in Crawfordsville last week and hiring a team from Insley & Darnall went to Alamo. Wm. Sheets was his driver and they started on their return from Crawfordsville about 7 o'clock. The terrific thunderstorm soon overtook them and about 8:15 o'clock they were climbing the long hill just this side of the old Hibernian mill. On their right was the wild wood which climbs the precipitous descent to the creek below and rising about the road shuts the view from the south. On their left was a long stubble field. The rain was descending in torrents and the road an angry brook through which the horse patiently plodded in the inky blackness. Suddenly, however, a bright and blinding light broke through the woods on the right similar in brilliancy to that of a burning flash light. Before the startled men and horses could

grasp an idea there shot them a huge ball of white fire with a rush like that of a mammoth sky rocket. From this huge ball of blazing light smaller balls continually broke off and exploded with a noise similar to a rattling discharge of musketry. The great ball shot toward the earth at an angle of perhaps 45 degrees and before they realized it it struck in about the middle of the field. There was an explosion resembling that of a cannon and at once all was inky darkness. The horses crouched to the earth paralyzed with fear and blinded. The men clutched each other and stared into the night seeing nothing but shaking with fear. The whole display had lasted but about three seconds but was one never to be forgotten. When gradually they were able to distinguish each other, and the horses, the men perceived that they were surrounded by a bank of thick suffocating smoke. The horses were urged forward and Yountsville was reached before a word was spoken. Mr. Carmichael told his story this morning and stated that his eyes were still suffering from the light. The horses stumbled all the way to town and frightened at every noise or flash of lighting. Mr. Carmichael is satisfied that a large and valuable aerolite fell within an hundred yards of him last night and declares that he would not undergo his experience for whole county. Mr. Insley took Mr. Sheets and drove to the scene of the fall to attempt to discover the treasure. Mr. Sheets talked with reluctance on the subject, he fearing, as he stated, that his veracity might be questioned. The aerolite is said to have been about the size of a beer keg and the small balls of fire which broke off from it about the size of half pint whisky bottles. J.J. Insley and several others made a trip to the neighborhood of the Hibernian mill on Friday to look for the aerolite which Messrs. Carmichael and Sheets had seen fall in a corn field the night before. The aerolite was not found but in about the center of the field was found a large hole. By the side of it were found two blue rabbits and several lovely pink snakes which looked as though someone had been trying to stamp them in the ground. The general contour of the pit formed by the falling meteor closely resembled that of a full blown bung hole.

PART VI

WABASH COLLEGE

WABASH COLLEGE

I n the heart of Crawfordsville and Montgomery County sits a jewel. It is the home of the Little Giants. Wabash College came into existence on November 21, 1832. The land the college sits on was donated by a man by the name of Williamson Dunn. Dunn had also donated land to build Hanover College, as well as Indiana University.

The school was created by nine men to be an institute of higher learning for this region of the state. They wanted a school to teach ministers and

Wabash Corner.
Photo by authors.

teachers. They were all relatively young men with high ambitions. In 1835, they purchased 160 acres from Ambrose Whitlock. They used this to create the beginnings of a full-fledged school, selling off most of the acres to get the funds to build a building they called the college. The first building used for the college was Forest Hall, made from lumber instead of stone to keep down costs at the new school. Forest Hall is the heart of the school and has been moved many times to remain usable by the school. The school has now moved to its current location from that original campus Forest Hall sat on. Of the three buildings that make up the Historic Corner of Wabash, only the home of Caleb Mills remains in its original location. Caleb Mills, one of the most well-known leaders of Wabash, started the very first class with the ringing of a bell. This same bell is still being used to welcome students as well as see them off at graduation all these many years later. Wabash likes to keep its history and traditions alive and well even to this day.

THE MALL

The college has lots of stories about strange things happening. Even the Mall in the center of the college has had its fair number of stories. One such story tells of a monstrous sound coming from the Mall. It seemed to be as loud as "a Titan of old" and was terrifying to hear.

Crawfordsville Weekly Review, *February 2, 1884*
A Haunted Square
The College Campus is haunted by a spirit of no mean proportions and from the noise it makes is a general terrifier. Several parties have heard the groans of this bold spirit on different occasions and it had the effect of causing their hair to lift the hat from their head each time. It prowls about near the hour of midnight and utters groans of a most fiendish character. They appear to come first from the sky, then from under the earth, then off at a distance, sounding like a colossal snore made by a Titan of old then changing from a deep bass to a sharp rasping sound like drawing a file over the teeth of a cross cut say. It is no hoax, as several who heard it can testify.

THE PIONEER CHAPEL

The Pioneer Chapel was first opened on January 10, 1929. It was the first building on the Mall of the college that was built in the Georgian style. It was dedicated to the pioneers of Indiana. The opening of the chapel caused a major shift on the campus. Before that, the buildings faced the Arboretum. The chapel is where the students come for the beginning of their college life and where they end when they graduate.

The Pioneer Chapel. *Photo by authors*.

Inside the Pioneer Chapel. *Photo by authors.*

The chapel has been the center of campus and the center of a lot of the strange happenings on campus. A figure—some say it is a man—is seen on the second story. He seems to not like people to visit the chapel. He has been known to push people and yell at them to get out. He seems to have dark intentions toward those unlucky enough to come across him.

One story of the chapel comes from a custodian of the college who in years past was in the building cleaning, as was her normal routine. She was up on the second level when she felt like someone was trying to push her over the railing. This scared her, but thinking that it was all her imagination, she continued with her duties. A short time later, she heard her name yelled out and a hateful-sounding voice telling her to get out. It was extremely early in the morning at this time, and she knew the building was empty and that no living human voice was saying this. The custodian quickly left the building, but every time she was asked to clean the chapel after, she requested someone go in with her so as not to be alone.

LILLY LIBRARY

In 1959, Lilly Library opened up to the campus. It would take over from Yandes Hall as the library on campus and gave the students much more space for studying. It is a beautiful building, especially the doors of the archives. It is also the creepiest building on campus. The library gives all those who enter it strange vibes.

Many have said that a dark mass seems to float around both the third floor and the basement. When seen on the third floor, it doesn't seem to do much more than watch, but in the basement other things have been known to happen. The shelves are built to move but can be locked into place. It is always dangerous though to move between them without something holding them open. They are known to try to close on people, even with the brake set in place. The books on the shelves in the basement have been known to fly off the shelves toward people. If you happen to come across the black mass, it is suggested you immediately leave before you are hurt.

A custodian from many years ago was cleaning the basement when he felt someone watching him. Being an older gentleman, he was fairly familiar with the things that liked to torment people in the library. He had been cleaning it for several years and didn't bother with even turning the lights on at this point. What he wasn't prepared for was that as he was sweeping the floors between the shelves, they would start to shut on him. He knew the stories but figured they were just tales people told. Luckily, he had a habit of placing his cleaning cart just inside the shelf row in case he needed something from it. The shelves banged against it, stopping them from closing further. He

Lilly Library. *Photo by authors.*

Lilly Library basement. *Photo by authors.*

quickly left the row, but the entity wasn't done with him yet, as he saw a black shape move from behind the shelf. Immediately, a book flew off the shelf toward him. The gentleman, having had enough for the evening, quickly left the building and from then on wouldn't clean the basement without first turning on the lights in the area.

Other former employees talk about furniture moving around by itself. While cleaning other parts of the building overnight, they heard the sound of something heavy being shifted on the upper floor and went to investigate. No one was around, but grooves in the carpet showed that a table, which would take a dozen people to even budge, was no longer sitting in its previous position. Without seeing this table for yourself, you might find it hard to believe someone hadn't just shifted it, but when the college needs this particular table moved, they must bring in reinforcements to get the job done.

DETCHON

Yandes Library Hall, or Detchon, as it is now called, has some interesting stories about it. It was built in 1890 as a gift from Simon Yandes to the college. The building is laid out in the form of a Latin cross. It was built in such a way to make it fireproof, according to the architect. The building stood as the campus library until Lilly Library was built. It was renamed the Detchon Center after a major remodel.

The Detchon Center seems welcoming when you come inside. It is a place where the college has lots of dinners and parties. However, sometimes things

Detchon. *Photo by authors.*

The Detchon elevator. *Photo by authors.*

get a little strange. The elevator seems to move on its own, and sometimes when you walk into the building, you can hear people talking and laughing or even someone calling your name to join the party, even though the building will be empty at the time. A child is sometimes seen and heard moving around the building, and fingernails are heard running across the chalkboards. Detchon is a place on campus where no matter the time of night or how empty the building may actually be, you never quite feel alone.

One night, a few years ago, a young custodian was taking a break and sitting in the chairs near the elevator playing on his phone. He had been cleaning the building for a while that night and had become familiar with the sounds and other things that happened in the building. That night, though, things got alarming for him. The elevator door opened, and immediately, he heard his name called, followed by someone asking him to join them. He immediately left the building and the job soon after.

CALEB MILLS HOUSE

C aleb Mills was the very first member of the Wabash faculty. He was the "Father of the Indiana Public School System" and worked his whole life to improve the teaching of education. He came to Crawfordsville in 1833 with his wife, Sarah. He was a graduate of Dartmouth College. He was the first professional teacher and president of Crawfordsville Classical High School before the name was changed to Wabash College.

His original class was only twelve students. He taught all the classes himself and was also the minister of the church. In 1854, he earned the position of Indiana superintendent of public instruction in a reasonably close race.

Caleb Mills House. *Photo by authors.*

Inside the living room of Caleb Mills and the mysterious painting. *Photo by authors.*

Professor Mills remained at Wabash until his death in 1879. He and his wife built the Caleb Mills House in 1836, and he lived there throughout the remainder of his days. The house was left to the college in 1926, and it served the college in several different roles until the modern day.

The house is a place for small gatherings as well as a small hotel. People say they hear voices throughout the place; they feel like they are not alone or are being watched. The painting in the living room scares people the most because they feel like the eyes follow them everywhere around the room. If you look at it from the side, it seems to change to a skeleton instead of the way it looks normally. It is kind of an initiation to the Wabash crew of workers to be told the story of the picture and how it changes when looked at. The team member is given the task of cleaning the building, and many have an experience directly after their first time working in it, be it the painting changing on them or hearing some strange noise in the building.

LAMBDA CHI ALPHA

One of the oldest houses on campus is the Crawford home that Lambda Chi Alpha fraternity inhabits. They made this house their own in the early years of the twentieth century and never looked back. The house was rumored to be a location for the Underground Railroad, and at least one of the former inhabitants passed away on the premises. Lambda Chi has a rich history on the campus. It is the largest fraternity on campus and seems to have members from every sport, club and group.

Lambda Chi Alpha. *Photo by authors.*

Lambda Chi Alpha stairs. *Photo by authors.*

THE GHOST OF CLARA CRAWFORD
WANDERS THIS HOUSE
IN SEARCH OF A FAMILIAR SIGHT
THIS PORTION OF THE
ORIGINAL BANNISTER MAY
SERVE TO PUT HER AT EASE
ON A DARK AND STORMY NIGHT
HER HAND MIGHT BE SEEN
HOLDING THIS BANNISTER AS SHE
DID ON THE EVE OF HER DEATH

Left: A piece of the railing and plaque. *Photo by authors.*

Right: The plaque. *Photo by authors.*

They also have the most well-known history when it comes to the paranormal. They have a resident spirit or ghost by the name of Clara Crawford. Clara is believed to have died in the house during a storm and can often be seen still wandering around the house. Her presence is mostly felt around the stairwell when you first enter the building, as it was on this stairwell that she met her final moments. A piece of the banister from the original works is still on display to help calm her spirit, and a plaque tells the story. Many have said she makes sure that the boys know of her presence and they remain good Wabash gentlemen and do not do anything she would disagree with.

TAU KAPPA EPSILON

Tau Kappa Epsilon, or TKE as it is known in Crawfordsville, was founded in 1927. It moved to its current building after its construction in 2008. TKE was the first racially integrated fraternity on campus and has maintained its tradition of diversity. In 1936, after several years of decrease in enrollment, the fraternity was forced to close, but it restarted in 1962. TKE was the first fraternity to outlaw hazing in all its chapters around the world.

Tau Kappa Epsilon. *Photo by authors.*

TKE has an interesting history of things happening in the fraternity house, but the most recent stories stand out the most. The doors seem to have begun opening and slamming closed, and some claim that often it feels like the door is being ripped from your hand as you touch it. The tables and chairs move around on their own and refuse to stay how they are placed. The strangeness only seems to grow with each year. Some alumni can be heard to say that perhaps Potato, a former fraternity brother, has returned after his passing to have fun with his brothers in the home he loved most.

GOODRICH HALL

Goodrich Hall was opened in 1939. It was a gift from James Putnam Goodrich, a trustee at the time. He had made a bet that he would pay for the building if the college maintained a budget and didn't go over it for three years. This was especially hard because it took place during the Great Depression, but people tightened their belts and took extreme cuts to make it happen. Goodrich is home to more than just the physics and math departments; it is also home to some interesting experiences.

Goodrich. *Photo by authors.*

The phenomenon seems to be innocent in nature, simply opening doors and cabinets, as well as slamming doors that are left opened. One day though, while an employee was cleaning the building, something happened to startle her. The custodian was cleaning when a door opened in front of her. This was strange, as these doors can't move on their own, even with a strong wind, and the building was completely empty. She no sooner went through the door than it closed behind her. Was something trying to help her as she was cleaning or just making its presence known to her?

HOVEY COTTAGE

Hovey Cottage was built in 1837 by Otis Hovey. Hovey was one of the reasons the college is what it is today. He convinced his closest friend, Caleb Mills, to come teach at the school. Hovey was more than just one of the founders of the college; he was the heart of the school. His house was left to the college in 1898 and was moved from its original location to allow space for the Kane House to be built. It was moved again in 1965 to its current location. It serves as an office building for the college.

Hovey Cottage on the left and Forest Hall on the right. *Photo by authors.*

The building is small but has a big personality, and the upstairs can give off some creepy feelings. People have been known to tell stories of being pushed and feeling like something wanted them to leave. There are even stories of people being pushed down the stairs. One such story comes from a young man who was at the top of the stairs when all of a sudden, he felt hands on his back. A quick shove, and the young man was halfway down the stairs before regaining his balance. Why something dislikes having people upstairs we might not know, but it is something to be careful of if you visit.

ARNOLD HOUSE

The Schroeder Center for Career Development, better known as Arnold House, has some strange stories about it as well. The upstairs can get pretty scary if you are there alone. Spend a lot of time there, and you can even start to wonder if you are going crazy. The upstairs seemingly will mess with your balance as you walk around the building. A lot of employees won't enter the building alone, especially at night. The hairs on

The Arnold House. *Photo by authors*.

your limbs immediately stand straight up when you enter the building alone, and you have a feeling someone is watching you. You can smell cigarette smoke even though no one is in the building. The doors will open and close around you, and even though the floors are carpeted, you can hear footsteps from upstairs. This building is not for the faint of heart.

Some workers believe when they smell coffee or cigarette smoke coming from nowhere that Ronald, a former employee who was well loved, has decided to come into work. The presence upstairs is at its worst directly in the center of the building and is like a magnet that draws your attention when you come in. The building's upstairs floor plan is very different in design and tends to creep out even the strongest-willed person.

CONCLUSION

Crawfordsville may be a small city, but it has a wondrous past that piques the interest and sparks a thrill among the paranormally curious. Whether you believe in these stories or not, this town has a rich history of believing, and these stories are the inheritance of the residents. Though the characters in these tales may have passed on, they will never truly be gone, as the citizens continue to share them. If you have stories that you didn't see within these pages and you'd like to share them, please send them to cville_paranormal_society@yahoo.com or visit legendsloreandhauntings.com.

SOURCES

Sources for this book include many newspapers and periodicals published in Crawfordsville and other parts of the state. Each source is cited individually in the chapters. Individuals who helped or provided information about the history of Crawfordsville are cited in the acknowledgements. Interviews were conducted with many individuals who wished to have their names withheld, and that was granted.

Crawfordsville Daily Journal, January 28, 1890; September 5, 1891; September 7, 1891; July 7, 1892.

Crawfordsville District Public Library. www.cdpl.lib.in.us.

Crawfordsville Review, January 8, 1870; February 11, 1871; June 14, 1890; October 29, 1892.

Crawfordsville Weekly Journal, October 14, 1869; February 2, 1884; April 1, 1893.

Daily Argus, October 21, 1892.

Daily Democrat, January 25, 1869.

Daily Journal, October 20, 1892; October 22, 1892.

Doubt, the Fortean Society Magazine. N.d.

Facebook. "Montgomery County History and Folklore." www.facebook.com/MCHistoryandFolklore.

Fort, Charles. *LO!* N.p.: Claude Kendall, 1931.

Gaddis, Vincent. *Mysterious Fires and Lights.* New York: D. McKay Co., 1967.

Indianapolis Journal, October 17, 1885.

Jefferson Daily Evening News, November 11, 1885.

Journal of Magellan's Voyage. From the account of Antonio Pigafetta. N.p., 1522.

Montgomery County, Indiana. www.ingenweb.org/inmontgomery.

National UFO Reporting Center. nuforc.org.

Newport Hoosier State, October 28, 1885.

New York Times, October 17, 1885.

Sacramento Daily Union, October 31, 1891.

Sugar Creek Players. www.sugarcreekplayers.org.

This Is Indiana. thisisindiana.angelfire.com.

Wabash. www.wabash.edu.

ABOUT THE AUTHORS

C hristopher Hunt has always had a passion for the paranormal, cryptids and ancient history. He co-founded the Crawfordsville Paranormal Society, where they look into the real history and scientific data around paranormal activities and legends within Montgomery County, with his wife and friends. He resides in Crawfordsville with his wife and her horde of animals.

C hristina Hunt has worked with the public library system for over twenty-three years. Storytelling, often referred to as "porch sitting," has always been a big part of her family, and ghost stories and spooky tales were always the best part. She continues the tradition with her younger siblings, nieces and nephews whenever possible. She resides in Crawfordsville with her husband, three dogs and a cat named Turtle.